BRAINROT

THE GEN-A SLANG LEXICON

OHIO RIZZLER

ELEVATED
PUBLISHING

INTERNAL MEMORANDUM

Policy number: OLC-LANG-RIZZ

Effective Date: 11/11/24

Owner: The Office of Language Compliance

Description: The Gen-A Youth Adaptation and Translation Taskforce (GYATT)

1. PURPOSE

Our workspace has time and again honored the tenets of diversity and inclusion in hopes of creating a harmonious environment where people of all ages, backgrounds, and races can come together, collaborate, and bring their best energy forward.

2. SCOPE

Keeping in line with our goals, we want to bring your attention to our 'GYATT Initiative.' In the coming weeks, you will notice an influx of new team members. These new members of our team are the result of hiring for this initiative conducted by our Office of Language Compliance.

3. DEFINITIONS

- **GYATT.** As you might have noticed, we already used this term in the memo. Originating from rich African American Vernacular English (AAVE), the word has gone through a semantic shift in the 2020s, and where once it served as a euphemism for Goddamn, it is now a two-fold exclamation that still retains its original meaning while also coming into its own as a noun that refers to a person with a large derriere. While multifunctional in that it can be used as to express excitement, shock, and happiness, we advise that you reserve this word for guttural reactions only. Use sparingly unless you want to be called up to HR.

- **Rizz.** Short for charisma, this term provides credibility, acknowledgement, and peer respect if you possess it. Those who possess more rizz than average are termed as Rizzlers and tend to fare better in life, meetings, and impromptu Zoom calls.
- **Aura.** This replacement term for vibe comes in with a built-in numerical system. If your aura is positive, then it will be off the charts and somewhere in the hundred thousands. You might see it represented in your next performance review report as +100,000 aura. However, say you accidentally spill coffee on the CEO's favorite coat, or show up to work late consecutively, then you will be deducted -999,9999 aura points.
- **NPC.** Failure to integrate with colleagues, interact authentically with them, and bring value to the company will relegate you to the title of NPC. A Non-Playable Character is someone who is bland, repetitive, and operates in a dull, mechanical, uninspiring way. If you do not excel at work and instead go through the motions, you shall be deemed an NPC.
- **Let Him Cook.** When someone excels at work, performs at their maximum level, they cook. And

when you want to encourage someone's performance, the appropriate phrase is, "Let him/her/them cook!" Do not interrupt these maestros when they are at work. Do not question them. Just sit back and appreciate their brilliance.

- **GOAT.** The Greatest of All Time is a phrase reserved for those rizzlers who have maximum aura and cook all the time. See? You are getting the hang of it. They are the ones who when they step into the room, you have no other option but to cry out, "Gyatt!" Our honorable CEO, who pulled himself by the bootstraps and made a company out of scratch, the same man who pays all our salaries with benefits and dentals, is an example of a GOAT.
- **Skibidi.** While we are not exactly sure of what it means, this word is multifaceted in that it can mean something good, bad, or strange depending upon the context.

4. POLICY

The future is now, and unfortunately for some of us, it speaks a different language. A language that is not rooted in the jargon of the previous century. The language of tomorrow has arrived, and our younger counterparts, Generation Alpha, are already speaking it fluently.

They are not charismatic; they possess rizz. They do not vibe; they calculate aura. Their idea of excellence is not confined to performance reviews and outmoded metrics. It instead is measured on a non-conventional spectrum ranging from Skibidi to GOAT.

For all of you perplexed by the sudden shift in language, we encourage you to reach out to the individuals mentioned above interspersed within the office. They are the Gen-A Youth Adaptation and Translation Taskforce (GYATT), and they will help you differentiate fanum tax from that of your capital gains.

Effective immediately, all employees must familiarize themselves with the latest dialect. You may have only recently become familiar with that of the generation before theirs; however, it is with great importance that the culture we strive for continues to adapt. Just as we have transitioned from millennial-speak to that of Gen-Z, we must continue to do so as language further evolves.

To maintain intergenerational synergy in and outside the workplace, all interactions must reflect an understanding of these new terms. Failure to work towards a satisfactory level of communication with this generation, as determined by the company, may result in a change of your flair and/or pronouns to begin displaying as NPC. With continued non-compliance and escalation of your NPC performance improvement plan, disciplinary action will result in aura deduction, up to and including exile to Ohio. While this is not a literal exile, and for reasons currently unclear, this is considered to be purgatory. More information on the specifics of these disciplinary actions will be disseminated by leadership as this progressive discipline policy evolves.

Effective immediately, we will begin weekly cultural and inclusion training of which will be primarily focused on this evolution of language. Leadership does understand that this may not be an effective use of time for our new-hire employees given the topic of discussion, but this training is mandatory for all employees. We feel that we can only foster this change when all are included.

In anticipation of these weekly meetings, an e-book has been attached. It is expected of all employees to have reviewed this information prior to the initial meeting, which will be scheduled at a time to be determined during the next week.

5. CHANGES

Please note that we have also retired the following decidedly outdated slang:

a. YOLO
b. LOL
c. Bae
d. Yeet
e. Finesse
f. Noob

Usage of this and any slang added to this list, as determined by the company, moving forward, is strictly prohibited.

5. DISCLOSURE

We are a private employer, and are therefore not subject to the restrictions of the first amendment.

6. WAY FORWARD

To assist you better in your learning process, we have compiled a non-exhaustive glossary of must-know terms. The knowledge of these terms and your proficiency in using them will be evaluated during your next performance review, so we recommend you familiarize yourself with them accordingly.

Equipped with this knowledge, we encourage you to go forth and engage with your Gen-A colleagues. Remember, this is more than just a language shift. It is a cultural evolution. If you ever feel lost, just refer back to this guide. Or better yet, ask the chat.

The key to surviving in this ever-changing, meme-driven world is to embrace the new slang. If you have any questions, a GYATT representative will be directed to your cubicle to assist you with this new vernacular.

If all else fails, pretend you're from Ohio.

6. CONTACT INFORMATION

None. We will not field any input regarding this change in cultural language.

ONE

AURA

THE CURRENCY OF COOL

THE NOTION of non-monetary currency denoting someone's standing in society has always been prevalent across different cultures. Those at the top of the pyramid are labeled cool, and those at the bottom of this societal structure are labeled uncool.

THE EVOLUTION OF LABELS AND ARCHETYPES

I am assuming it goes back to caveman times. Think of the guy who invented fire. He must have been the hot shit, the topic of every conversation around the watering hole.

Or, if you're looking for a more relevant example, think of the Marlboro Man. For some of you, the term may be as alien as the brand Marlboro itself. Still, there used to be a time when the epitome of ruggedness, masculinity, and toughness was embodied in the form of the Marlboro Man–a lone gunslinger riding his horse along a ranch, jaw chiseled like that of a Greek God, smoking away Marlboro cigarettes effortlessly.

At that time (this is the 20th century we're talking about), you had Clint Eastwood, John Wayne, Sam Elliot, and Gary Cooper whom embodied those features, and, as such, were praised as cultural heroes donned in cowboy hats, cigars, and cool.

Precursors to your Arnold Schwarzenegger and Sylvester Stallone's Action Hero archetypes, which became more prominent in the 80s and 90s and fizzled out with the advent of the 21st century, handing over the reins to a new type of hero. The superhero. The caped crusaders. The vigilantes who rise above mediocrity and do good in the name of justice and altruism. As it happens, we're currently living in an era where every other movie that has been premiered is about Iron Man, Dr. Strange, Thor, Captain America, Spiderman, you name it.

Much like the cultural evolution of the hero archetype in modern media, the currency that connotes coolness has also evolved drastically, as has its phraseology.

In a not-so-distant past, the term nerd was a derogatory one designated to the acne-marked, big-glasses-wearing, skinny freaks of nature who assembled in the A/V room after school and played Dungeons and Dragons with the rest of their kind. These social pariahs were in stark contrast to the jock archetype, who were handsome, well-built, charismatic, got all the girls, and were on the fast-track to success with their sports scholarships and their promising futures.

But somewhere between the 90s and the late 2000s, nerds reinvented themselves to the point that it's cool to be one nowadays. Hell, you'll find people from the jock archetype literally migrating toward the previously unpopular archetype. Henry Cavill, for instance, the buff, muscular British actor who portrayed Superman and the Witcher, has stuck the title of nerd to his chest and puffed it proudly as the badge of honor it is, citing Warhammer 40k and PC building as his niche interests.

One video of him dressed in a vest, assembling a gaming PC, did more for the entire demographic of PC gamers than years of technological advancement at Intel or Nvidia.

Today, we're living in an era called the nerd-renaissance, with Dungeons and Dragons adaptations coming out the wazoo, niche comic books being turned into movies and TV shows, and AAA games being released to mass fanfare and critical acclaim —all of which is no longer a fringe culture but mainstream culture that everyone partakes in thanks to easy accessibility.

When cultures (including pop culture) evolve, so does language, and this shift in language is derived from newer generations adopting new terms to refer to phenomena as old as humanity itself. Whether or not they were called that, there were always rizzlers. And even though it was known by a different name, aura was always the factor that decided which table you sat at during lunch at school.

DEFINITION

Aura refers to the "it" factor that someone exudes. It's a word used to describe someone's social energy, the presence they embody, and the charisma they possess. Someone with a positive aura is a confident and attractive person to be around. Someone with a negative aura is a socially clueless, awkward person.

EXAMPLES

Imagine you're walking down the street, and the universe suddenly decides to punish you for existing. You trip on a crack in the pavement and fall face-first, the bag of bagels coming loose and scattering all over the sidewalk. On top of the bagels and the coffee you spilled, you have also lost 10,000 Aura Points.

This social credit system goes beyond just docking your points for being uncool. Suppose you help your friend out in a time of need. Maybe they're short on cash, and you lend them some rather generously. You'd gain 20,000 aura points for being a mensch.

Pull off a great outfit, save a friend from embarrassment, or post a TikTok dance that's super hard to pull off, and you'll win aura.

Make a klutz out of yourself, fail terribly at rizz publicly, or do something unethical that earns you the ire of the people, you'll lose aura. Lose enough aura, and you'll be banished to Ohio, where the rest of the outcasts live out their canceled lives.

But if you think of it as a metric, then know that there is another way to gain and lose aura. These days, very hyper-specific memes carry captions like "If you received this meme, you lose 100,000 aura, and if you're the one sending this meme, you gain 100,000 aura." It's like a virtual game of tag, and you're it.

ORIGINS

Regarding origins, it's derived from video games that feature characters like Goku, who seem to exude a powerful aura.

Its recent precursor was the social credit meme that poked fun at the Chinese social credit system. You might have seen that video of John Cena eating an ice-cream and speaking Chinese whilst promoting one of his movies. The joke is that John Cena is gaining a million social credits in China.

At the end of the day, it's just light-hearted fun where your social wins and fails are given a playful scoring system. There's no actual registry keeping count of your score, so even if you lose aura every now and then, you can relax. You can redeem yourself by pulling off one of those Fortnite dances.

TWO

BRAINROT

FOR WHEN THE DIGITAL DECAY SETS IN

BRAINROT IS the consequence of being perpetually online. While a lot of us have to stay online or on our computers for work, study, or even entertainment, there is a fine difference between regular fatigue and brainrot.

DEFINITION

You see, brainrot happens when you lose all sense of who you are, where you are, and how you are. It's the stage of mental deterioration that you reach when you have consumed so much internet content—ranging from Twitch streams to TikTok infinite scroll short-form videos—that your brain feels fried.

The overwhelming sensation exhibits itself in the form of erratic and irritative behavior. It becomes a case of monkey see, monkey do, and soon enough, the brainrotten person in question starts to speak only in niche slang, begins to behave in the exaggerative way that streamers and content creators do, and becomes downright unpleasant in the way a person undergoing withdrawal becomes when their internet connection is taken away.

Their mind becomes so saturated with viral videos, internet slang, and content loops that it becomes impossible for them to think outside of the confines of it. That eventual plateau of mental degeneration, where one has officially crossed over from sanity to psychosis, is called brainrot.

Much like a lot of things that are not taken seriously by the younger generation (as is the case with everyone who is in their teens), the phenomenon of brainrot, albeit quite considerably a grave phenomenon that is linked to mental health disorders such as ADHD, virtual autism, and antisocial behavior, is made light of. And so, the brain-fog that sets in as a result of internet scrolling, streaming, gaming, online interaction, and content consumption is regarded with frivolity rather than seriousness.

One can argue that given the frequency of the usage of the term amongst Gen-A, the word brainrot is being interchangeably used with phrases such as "I've been on the computer for too long" or "I've been using my phone more than usual" but in a more dramatic and exaggerative way, because what is Gen-A if not a little hyperbolic?

ORIGINS

The origins of this term can be traced back to covidian times. In the early 2020s, what with the strict rules set in place to curtail the pandemic, millions, if not billions, of people found themselves under lockdown, and with such limited avenues at their disposal, many of them turned to the internet to entertain themselves. It just so happened that the generation that happened to be entertaining themselves the most were the teens and younger kids who had become accustomed to the readily available internet access. Think about it. They had to use the internet for online classes on Zoom. For making assignments. For getting in touch with friends. And just about everything else, from Roblox and Fortnite to keeping up with the latest trends on social media.

While covid itself, the subsequent enforced restrictions, and figure heads suggesting the injection of bleach were all a catalyst, they were hardly the whole picture. Brainrot is a reflection of the digital age, where Gen-A grew up with screens in their hands in the form of tablets, smartphones, and gaming consoles. The obsessive overuse of such devices is attributed to their ease of use and intuitive design.

In the olden days, millennials (dubbed the boob-tube generation) had, what, a central TV, a desktop computer, and a landline? As technologically marvelous as it was at that time, it still was difficult for someone to use these technologies on a continuous basis. In the days of CRT monitors, you quite literally could not sit in front of a screen for long before it started to burn your eyeballs and cause severe strain and headaches. If your grandma called to talk to you, your speakers would hiss and your internet connection dropped. Nowadays, with your latest eye-friendly AMOLEDs, such restrictions have been lifted, and you can keep staring at a screen for as long as you want without straining your eyes as much.

But with Gen-A, this was not the case. Unlike Gen-Z, who saw the rapid development of such technology in their childhood, Gen-A (born between 2010 to 2025) opened their eyes in a world where tech like smartphones, social media apps, lightning-fast internet connections, high-power PCs, cutting-edge gaming consoles were the norm rather than the exception. And so, with generational tech literacy helping them out in figuring out how to avail this tech, it was only a matter of time before some of them started to overuse it. Still, with all of this technology, computer literacy and typing speed sunk to the depths.

To be honest, it's not entirely a case of "this younger generation is doomed, and our days were better!" Brainrot, while a popular term, remains a relatively rare phenomenon, and the fact that Gen-A itself has a slang term for such a condition reflects their self-awareness.

EXAMPLES

If you find yourself overusing phrases such as sigma, mogging, looksmaxxing, rizz, and skibidi (especially skibidi, along with its variation of skibidi toilet), then there's a good chance that the prevalent internet culture has seeped into your brain and has affected the way you interact with your world.

It's when you find yourself doing a really niche trend TikTok dance out in public even though there's no camera recording your actions. Do you remember the days when anime had done a number on every teen's psyche, and they were going about running like Naruto and talking amongst each other like they were animated characters out of a manga? That's also a variation of brainrot ascribed to anime culture.

There's another variation of brainrot called gooning, wherein a person becomes so obsessed with readily available internet porn that their entire existence boils down to the cycle of sexual stimulus and climax to the point that that's all they care about.

CAN BRAINROT BE CURED?

Fortunately, yes. There is an easy fix for it.

There are a few tried and tested ways—that are the equivalent of hangover fixers—which work remarkably well, and Gen-A being Gen-A has turned even those fixes into memes.

1. **Touch Grass.** This phrase is both a meme and leetspeak for when you want someone delusional to go out and reacquaint themselves with reality, and also a beneficial remedy to quickly get over brainrot. Touching grass refers to taking a break from the internet, going outside, and getting in touch with nature as a way to cure their screen-time-induced malaise. The therapeutic quality of touching literal grass is known to alleviate the symptoms of brainrot.

2. **Limit Screen Time.** It's pretty understandable that you cannot outright cut out screen time from your life, so how about setting boundaries for how long you spend on social media, the internet, and gaming? There are several apps that help you monitor your screen time and limit your internet usage, which you can use to take a break every now and then and keep the rot at bay.

3. **Engage in Offline Activities.** A smoother way to heal yourself from brainrot is engaging in offline activities like reading books, going to the gym, or having a conversation with a friend or family member that doesn't involve quoting memes.

4. **Digital Detox.** A complete digital detox that involves turning off your phone, avoiding social media,

and disconnecting from the internet entirely for a day or two.

Next time you feel like you've been afflicted with endless content-fueled brain haze, remember that you're not alone. There's a whole internet out there with brain-rot-addled chronically online users spam commenting skibidi in the chat.

Welcome to the rot where the memes are endless, the cringe is real, the content is chaotic, and your brain cells are collateral damage.

THREE

YOU ARE THE MAIN CHARACTER, THE CHAT, AND THE NON-PLAYABLE CHARACTER

I KNOW this is something that sounds like the Gen-A reincarnation of Rumi would say, but these are very real terms that are used every day by the younger generation, and there's a profound meaning behind each of them. It may not be as profound as Sufi metaphysics, but it is still close enough.

It's important for us to realize that Gen-A, like every generation before and after them, goes through the motions of the human condition. Grief, joy, sadness, desires—they felt the entire spectrum of emotions and feelings out there. It's just that sometimes, those emotions get amplified because of the different avenues of self-exploration they have.

Twitch, for instance, the streaming website with hundreds of thousands of content creators streaming videogame playthroughs, social media commentary, bubble baths in inflatable pools (yes, for the exact reason you're thinking why), and straight-up shenanigans that involve jumping over Ferraris (do NOT try that at home, because the streamer who pulled that stunt off has been banned from Twitch for life, and also, duh, because it is fatal!), can be summed up as the modern human experience amplified, broadcasted, documented, and assimilated with millions of viewers partaking in that human experience.

You've probably heard phrases like "He's giving main character energy," or "she's such an NPC," or even more specifically, someone referring to their peers as "chat" in an ironic capacity.

What does it all mean, and how does it tie in with Nicki Minaj and Christiano Ronaldo?

CHAT: YOU'RE THE AUDIENCE

Imagine a really popular Twitch streamer. Let's take the poster-boy of Twitch, Kai Cenat, who started streaming straight-up comedy and has now become one of the biggest names on Twitch. His presence is so massive that he's got famous people like Nicki Minaj and 21 Savage on his livestreams, sitting right alongside him in his home like they were just friends hanging out. Of course, they were there to promote their albums and gain more online traction, but still. It goes to show that the whole guest-coming-over-at-late-night-show model is going to be slowly replaced by livestream appearances and podcasts.

Anyways, back to the point. When someone such as Kai Cenat streams, they're not doing it in the void. They've got hundreds of thousands of viewers interacting with the streamer through the live-chat. That's where the term comes from.

In Gen-A terminology, chat is the loyal, semi-anonymous, online following around you that's there to comment, interact and hype you up. The term has evolved beyond just streaming usage. If you're on Reddit or X (previously known as Twitter) or Facebook (remember that relic of the past?), you'll find comments in the vein of, "Chat, is this guy capping?" or the more commonly used "F's in the Chat."

When a content creator interacts with their audience and calls them *chat*, there are two things at play. One, they're soliciting their viewer's attention, and two, they're establishing that they, the content creator in question, are the main character while the rest are just part of the background.

NON-PLAYABLE CHARACTER

If a collection of extras is called chat, then a single unit is referred to as a non-playable character. Deriving from videogames, the term draws a parallel between pre-programmed, humdrum background videogame characters and real-life people who behave so monotonously that they might as well be pre-programmed sheep in a videogame. Or the Matrix.

The derogatory term for a character that follows preset scripts, utterly devoid of any original action, and so ignominious in their mediocrity that they blend in with the background should, by all means, come across as an insult, right?

And yet, surprisingly, in a bid to embrace the ironic, content creators on TikTok came up with the NPC trend where they do live streams and behave like videogame side-characters, repeating onerous phrases, making repetitive motions, and acting bizarrely for the benefit of the audience. Though, how the audience benefited from it remains unclear to this day.

The content creators who jumped on that brief bandwagon cashed in hard and became immensely rich as a result of digital gifts, which are worth real money, bestowed upon them by the masses who thought they were manipulating these creators with gift-based prompts. For instance, an ice-cream emoji gift cost a certain amount of cents, and whenever the emoji would pop up on the screen, the content creator would go, "Ice cream so good, Ice cream so good, yummy yummy in my tummy!" To get more of that surrealness, people would send more gifts just to get the same reaction over and over.

In the end, it was the content creators manipulating their viewers and not the other way around because they were the ones who cashed out with hundreds of thousands of dollars. And here we are, busting our buts on our 9-to-5s, thinking that our hard work justifies the very finite amount of money we make when all it takes is to become an online NPC, make a fool of yourself in front of your viewers, and rake in hundreds of thousands of dollars such as in the case of creators like Pinky-Doll (yes, that's a real person), who reportedly made $7,000 a day acting as the internet's puppet.

Besides the cultural phenomenon it became, the term can be used as a stinging critique, implying that a person lacks depth or individuality. A person so mediocre that they are not a protago-nist or side-character but a background character.

A somewhat accurate example of NPC in a sentence would be: "Can you believe Steve? Such an NPC with those two same plaid shirts and his lunchbox and thermos. He does the same thing every single day. How can you live like that?"

One can guess that since the oldest member of Gen-A is four-teen to fifteen years old, the realization hasn't settled on them that sooner or later, we all get into the monotonous rhythm of life in the name of responsibility and accountability.

No one sets out to be an NPC. Sometimes, it's life that turns even the most main character of all time into just a background actor.

MAIN CHARACTER ENERGY

Laced in equal parts irony and admiration, the term can mean one of two things.

It can refer to a person who wants to be the center of attention in a very narcissistic capacity, especially in situations that do not call for such behavior. Think of the rude, Bluetooth-in-the-ear monkey suit at the bank being loud and brash. That's a guy who thinks that the entire world is his oyster, including this middle-of-nowhere B of A branch. Or, a Karen, who self-righteously takes it upon herself to right the wrongs she's seeing in front of her by 'calling for the manager.' That's the main character energy that you do not want.

But then there's the person who is brimming with self-confidence, self-assurance, and treats everyone with dignity and familiarity. Someone who knows everything about everyone and interacts with them much like the main character of a videogame would with the other characters in a game. A person who, through his positive actions and his optimistic presence, brings out the best in others, and earns the attention of others as opposed to vying for it forcibly. That's the kind of main character energy that you do want.

In either case, a person who possesses main character energy comes into a room and holds court and feels comfortable being the center of attention.

Taken in a positive way, you can cultivate main character energy by prioritizing yourself instead of being an expendable character in someone else's story, especially if that someone else is not giving you the respect and time you need.

You can also build main character energy by being your authentic self instead of trying to jump on bandwagons and do what everyone's doing. Following the crowd is a telltale sign of someone with NPC energy. Someone with main character energy tends to march to the beat of their own drum and is comfortable with it!

In our performative era, where everything's recorded and broadcasted, these terms represent the gamification of life while also serving as social critique and a way to remain self-aware in an increasingly online world.

Don't be a chat member in someone else's Twitch stream.

Don't be an NPC in someone else's questline.

Live your best life, and make sure that you're the one running the show.

FOUR

LET HIM COOK
THE NONCULINARY ART OF KEEPING IT 100

IF YOU GOT the notion that this had something to do with firing up the ol' reliable grill, then you, my friend, are like me. An old timer.

This term has nothing to do with food. Instead, it's about giving someone space to work their magic when they're doing something out of the ordinary. It's about trusting that person's process, stepping back, and letting them have their moment. You'd use this term to stop others from interrupting someone's flow state. In the Gen-A circles (both online and IRL), this has become a supportive phrase.

It's about letting a main character harness positive aura by doing something skibidi, and you're probably reading this sentence, wondering to yourself how you were able to understand what it meant. That's the power of knowledge, and sometimes, knowledge comes in the shape and size of utterly inane slang with surprisingly positive meanings.

Such as letting someone cook.

ORIGINS

If you follow the NFL and are a fan of the Seattle Seahawks, then you might remember people using the phrase "Let Russ Cook" as a rallying cry to let Russell Wilson take control of the offense. While this was a sports metaphor, it slowly blended with internet culture when rapper Lil B (also known as The Based God) popularized the word 'cooking' as a metaphor for taking meticulous time and care to perfect something. In one of his videos tiled Lil B Based Cooking (Let That Boy Cook), he encouraged his audience to embrace their craft and allow others to do the same.

Over time, the meme gained traction and is now being used as very popular background audio for viral short-form videos where masters of their craft exhibit their adroitness online.

DEFINITION

"Let him cook" is a way to pause everyone and let the moment unfold naturally without interference.

It's a friend looking out for a friend and letting them have their moment. But it's also the soundtrack for trick shot compilations on TikTok, just like it's a barbaric yawp that calls for support and affirmation.

EXAMPLES

If your friend's at a house party during a Call of Duty multiplayer marathon, and he's deep in the zone, kicking ass and taking names, you tell everyone to let him cook so that he can keep on with his streak.

If your crush is performing an electric guitar solo and you see someone about to interrupt, you go, "Let her cook now, let her cook," to let the performance flow uninterrupted while also hyping her up and making her notice you.

But then, there's the negative connotation. The phrase is used to poke fun at someone for doing a terrible job at something. When someone fails publicly, it's followed by a "Who let bro cook?" or "Bro should never be allowed to cook again."

While it primarily remains the internet's way of rooting for chaos and brilliance, it's also used to admonish those who fail to capitalize on the moment when they're supposed to be cooking. It also results in them losing 999,999 aura points in front of everyone.

FIVE

EDGING
THE GEN-A'S EQUIVALENT OF ABSTINENCE LOOPHOLES

BEFORE I MUSTER up the courage to go down this unhinged rabbit hole with you, I have to tell you about an online movement called No Fap and the manosphere comprising of personalities like Andrew Tate.

ORIGINS

Let's be real. Teenagers are gullible, and they're more often than not looking for someone to look up to, someone who's not necessarily a parental figure but someone who's achieved something tangible in life and speaks to them in their language. Enter the manosphere, a most wretched part of the internet where much older men brainwash the young'uns at large with images of wealth, flashy cars, smoking babes (geez, like I didn't sound a thousand years old there myself), and a chiseled masculine figure.

Naturally, many boys find themselves in this part of the internet after scrolling for a long time, and it's such a rabbit hole of an algorithm that it immediately overfloods your feed with far-right propaganda if you only click on a couple of videos.

Now, since these figures have nothing original to say, they rip off their motivational speeches straight from stoic philosophy, telling impressionable kids to suppress their emotions and focus on the 'hustle.' The 'hustle' is this crazy concept that if you invest in crypto, start drop-shipping, or pick up any number of passive income streams such as social media influencing or online copy-writing, you will somehow become a millionaire with a Bugatti in x number of days. It's important to note that I do not have a Bugatti.

And the lie sells because the seller of this lie sits atop this exaggerated throne with fat stacks of cash, a couple of sports cars in their garage, and a hedonistic lifestyle featuring a lot of smoking, decadent eating, and copious amounts of drinking—and justifying this lifestyle by saying that "Since we put in the hours in our hustle and turned into self-made millionaires, we get to do this, and if you want to do this, buy our course and learn the trade secrets from us."

So, what you have, at the end of the day, are hundreds of thousands of impressionable teenage boys, all of them gathered in the echo chamber that is the group chat of the course they bought to get rich, listening to the same mantras echoed over and over.

Now, one of those mantras that has evolved into a movement of its own with over a million adherents on Reddit alone is that masturbation is bad. The pseudoscience that goes into these faux-motivational speeches is that if you masturbate, you suffer from a lack of confidence, low testosterone levels, weaker muscles and bones, and your 'beta' energy will repulse women because somehow they can just smell that right off the air.

A new archetype forms, this Herculean, muscular man who abstains from masturbation so that he can use the magical super-power of 'semen retention' to become a sigma class male, someone who can go deep into the forest armed with nothing but a self-fashioned wooden spear and come out victorious with an alligator skewered all because he didn't jerk off.

I'm not knocking on the whole No Fap movement. It has its merits in terms of helping the youth break free from porn addiction and all. I'm just trying to tell you how edging became a popular term.

DEFINITION

Considered to be the opposite of gooning, an activity where you resort to degeneracy by overindulging in pornography and self-pleasure, and a middle-ground between complete abstinence and chronic addiction, edging refers to bringing yourself to the brink of orgasm and then stopping just before you climax. Doing so helps one increase their sexual stamina (another feature of the sigma archetype), retain semen, and if or when they do decide to climax, their climaxes would be more powerful.

The term truly gained traction in the early 2020s when tangential terms like edger and edge-master came to the forefront of the internet vernacular. Various catchphrases and spam comments such as "I will aggressively edge to you," are quite common on TikTok and Instagram. The term is used in No Nut November memes as well. No Nut November is an entire month dedicated to abstaining from 'nutting' for prostrate health and men's health awareness. During this month, partakers refrain from masturbation. And if you want to take a guess as to which organization has an active hand (get it?) in promoting this month, what would your guess be?

That's right.

No Fap.

EXAMPLES

So, in 2022, the trailer for the live-action Dungeons and Dragons movie was released. The main character, portrayed by Chris Pine, is hilariously named Edgin. In the movie, he is Edgin the Bard. The meme community ran with it, using the name and the term as a euphemism for creating sexual tension.

The more you edge, the more stoic and spiritually powerful you are. So, someone saying, "I edge for eight hours straight to Goth Egg" (Goth Egg is an adult performer), they're praising themselves for their ability to refrain from orgasm for a long time. Of course, the duration of time is highly exaggerated. To show moral support and appreciation, one can say, "I edge to you," such as in the case of several content creators who say that they "aggressively edge to every follower they get." Whatever that means.

Another heinous and rather popular example of this phrase is "edging in the back of the class," in which the rest of the class refuses to acknowledge the fact that someone sitting in the back of the room is indulging in self-pleasure. A hyperbolically reprehensible scenario that is obviously not meant to be tried in real life turns into peak humor.

A more innocuous example of the word's usage would be when you're heating something in the microwave, and you turn it off just before the timer runs out. That would be you edging the microwave by robbing it of the opportunity to beep loudly at the end of the timer. FYI, most modern microwaves have the ability to turn the beeping off. Do this at your own risk if you live with an edge-lord.

If Shakespeare were alive today, he'd reframe his popular Hamlet quote, "To edge or not to edge, that is the question."

And if Mr. Willy Shaky P wants to become a sigma, he should most definitely edge. There's simply no question about it.

SIX

FANUM TAX

WHEN THE FRIES ARE CRISPIER ON THE OTHER SIDE

YOU ORDERED FRIES. Plain cut with salt and some spice sprinkled on top. But the gods of luck and fate have blessed you because, in that basket, there's a beautiful, deep orange curly fry. It's yours to relish. You do not want to order a whole basket of curly fries because why would you? You want regular fries with just the one curly fry. That's the dream. It's your way to break free from the monotony of eating plain fries. Instead, sometime in the middle of the meal, you pick up that curly fry, eat it, and bask in the difference in the taste and texture, concluding it is nothing if not heavenly.

But then your jackass friend comes and sits by your side, goes, "Ooh! Accidental curly fry! FANUM TAX!" and grabs that most rare of delicacies from your basket and eats it for himself.

The audacity.

He is dead to you from this day forth.

You can rob a man, but you may never take his curly fry.

And not, most certainly, in the name of whatever the hell Fanum Tax is.

DEFINITION

It's not an alien concept, just like none of the concepts we've discussed so far are. For every term that the Gen-A thinks is uniquely their own, there exists a term in the forgotten tomes of millennial and Gen-X slang. It's the same with Fanum Tax.

The concept of food tax is not a new concept. It's a classic older brother, dad, or girlfriend who didn't want any fries move where they take a bite out of your food in the name of food tax. Simple, harmless fun–of course depending upon how hungry both you and they are, and the subsequent size of the 'tax.' It could be any number between one french fry to a whole baker's dozen. God help them if they take your curly fry, though. That's when it stops being simple, harmless fun. I'm pretty sure wars have been started for less.

The reason this phrase blew to viral meme popularity has to do with the streamer Fanum, who popularized this term. It's because of the mass perception that a lot of teenagers and young adults like to say this phrase unironically, whereas the truth is that several young adults and teens do use it, but in a very ironic capacity. The phrase is the butt of jokes in TikTok parody videos, such as the Gen-A slang overload song called "Sticking Out Your Gyatt For the Rizzler," a parody of the song Ecstasy by Suicidal Idol.

If you want to go even deeper into the rabbit hole, the song Ecstasy (before it became viral thanks to all the parodies and background music usage on TikTok) is a song about a toxic lesbian relationship, but at this point, it's exclusively being used as a meme. We're very sorry, Ms. Idol. Sometimes, the internet is not quite sensitive to emotional subtleties.

ORIGINS

Earlier, I mentioned a streamer called Kai Cenat. He's one of the most popular streamers on Twitch—and is, in general, considered an internet personality. Well, there's more. He's part of a collective called AMP, or "Any Means Possible." AMP is a group of online streamers who've had a meaningful hand in shaping modern slang. They have contributed to widely-known internet pop-culture from memes to 'canon events,' in which famous YouTubers and streamers come together and make content together.

Fanum is one of the AMP streamers, and the reason why the term is named after him is because he runs from his room to another streamer's room and takes a bite out of their food rather aggressively.

EXAMPLES

Parents, if you hear your child say, "Hit her with the Fanum Tax," you can relax. There's no physical assault involved and you can still claim them as a dependent; they probably just want to share their friend's food. Other phrases that are used in the same vein include:

- "She Fanum Taxed my entire bag of chips!"
- "Yo, you already hit me with the Fanum Tax. I'm not giving you any more."
- "It's time to collect my Fanum Tax!"

And if anyone from Gen-A is reading this, we're on to you. As certified, experienced grown-ups, we're going to do what we always do with new stuff. We're going to use it wrong and use it embarrassingly till it isn't cool anymore. We did that with Face-book, dabbing, Snapchat, and those silly Fortnite dances. We're going to Fanum Tax the term Fanum Tax itself.

See? We made it uncool already. Try and stop us.

INTERNAL MEMORANDUM

Policy number: OLC-LANG-RIZZ

Effective Date: It's Giving Final Warning Vibes

Owner: The Office of Language Compliance

Description: GYATT Disciplinary Warning

1. SCOPE

It has come to our attention that certain employees are struggling to embrace the new linguistic standards set forth by the Gen-A Youth Adaptation and Translation Taskforce (GYATT).

This memo serves as a formal disciplinary warning to all employees who have failed to integrate this new dialect into their daily work interactions, meetings, and casual water cooler conversations.

Despite the multiple training sessions, it seems that a handful of you have neglected to actively participate in this evolutionary process. Let us remind you that failure to comply with GYATT's guidelines will result in significant aura deduction and possibly relegation to NPC status. In case of repeated offenses, you will most certainly be banished to Ohio.

That said, we understand that transitioning from saying LOL to Ijbol or swapping the term aura for vibe can be a very jarring process, but it is no excuse for continued use of outdated, outmoded vernacular such as YOLO, on fleek, and bae.

Our corporate culture thrives on adaptability and commitment to staying relevant. This includes keeping up with the language of our youngest team members.

2. NOTED VIOLATIONS

Overuse of Outdated Slang: Several employees have continued to pepper their conversations with phrases like "lit" and "no cap" despite the fire emoji and the term "all fax no printer" being readily available for public use.

Misuse of New Terms: Regardless of whether this misuse is deliberate or unintentional, some of you have used words like rizz and skibidi out of context, or worse, inappropriately.

Failure to Attend Training: It has been brought to our attention that a continuing number of employees have either entirely skipped the training sessions or slept through them. Attendance is mandatory, and so is participation.

Aura Negligence: Many employees are unaware that they have let their aura points slip into the negative millions by ignoring mogging protocols and refusing to let others cook. Your aura is your responsibility. Your employment depends on your aura.

3. CORRECTIVE MEASURES

Effective immediately, the following corrective measures will be implemented.

Aura Audit: Qualified members of GYATT will now conduct aura score reviews. Employees with negative aura points will be required to supplement their negative numbers by attending additional training seminars titled "Rizzing yourself back from the edge: Aura Recovery for NPCs."

Mogging Mentorship Programs: The employees who have repeatedly demonstrated poor understanding of mogging and aura calculations will be paired with a mogging mentor and a Gen-A liaison who will guide them and aid them in becoming a GOAT.

Immediate Language Compliance Check: All office communications are going to be monitored by GYATT for any infractions of the linguistic guidelines. Failure to adapt will lead to further disciplinary action.

4. CONCLUSION

This memo serves as a reminder to all employees that corporate compliance is no longer just about dress codes, time cards, and TPM reports. It's also about staying vernacularly relevant in a world where memes and slang evolve faster than you can say, "What the Sigma?"

Remember Pookie, if you're not slaying, you're straying.

SEVEN

GOAT

AND WE'RE NOT TALKING MUTTON

THERE ARE some words that land differently. I remember back in the 80s, when something was cool, it was disco. That phrase was dated even back then and fizzled out sometime during the 80s, only to be replaced by fresh, dope, and neat. Enter the 90s, and you got words like cool, awesome, funky, and rad. In the 2000s and early 2010s, you had lit and hype. And now, in the 2020s, you've got GOAT.

It's got nothing to do with barnyard animals. It's a title–a declaration of absolute greatness. The word itself is an acronym that stands for 'Greatest of All Time.' A phrase that was once confined to the realm of competitive greatness, particularly in sports, is now democratized by Gen-A . Everything is and can be the GOAT if it's the best. That pastrami sandwich you ate? If it was good, then it was goated. Your boss gave you a hefty bonus at the end of the year? What an absolute goat.

Who's that trip-trapping on my bridge?

Well, that's just the Three Billy Goats Gruff from the beloved Norwegian fairy tale.

ORIGINS

Funnily enough, the word itself is not new. It can be traced back to 1992 (back when even the parents of some of the Gen-A weren't conceived) when Lonnie Ali, wife of Muhammad Ali, registered G.O.A.T. Inc to manage her husband's intellectual properties. Muhammad Ali famously said, "To be a great champion, you must believe you are the best. If you're not, pretend you are. I am the greatest. I said that even before I knew I was." He became the embodiment of what it meant to be the GOAT long before the term turned into everyday slang.

But even before the acronym took root, you had some of the greatest players hailed by the title "Greatest of All Time." Babe Ruth. Rocky Marciano. Lebron James. Michael Jordon. Serena Williams. And if you want to know how this word trickled into the public consciousness, it's from sports. The massive fan following of Ronaldo and Messi, as well as the respective rivaling groups who both argue that one instead of the other is the GOAT, has contributed to the rise of the phrase and its subsequent de-sportification.

On the one hand, you have ESPN anchors saying Derek Jeter is the GOAT, and then, on the other hand, you have iShowSpeed literally yelling in the faces of his fans and strangers alike that Ronaldo is the GOAT. Whose GOAT implications carry more weight?

Sometimes, there's no way of telling what will become a very common slang term in the future. Back in 2000, LL Cool J released an album called G.O.A.T, drawing from Ali's legacy, but even way back then, he could not have known that the title of his album would gain traction twenty years later.

Leave it to kids on Twitch and TikTok to take something so formal and dignified and add it to their everyday lexicon.

DEFINITION

Everything and every one good is declared GOAT. That's it. That's the only qualifying metric. Whether it's music, sports, games, or memes, if something is outstanding, it's goated.

Sabrina Carpenter, the up-and-coming pop culture icon? She's a GOAT.

That Fortnite kill-streak your friend is on for the past half hour? That's a goated kill-streak.

The barista who makes excellent espresso at your local coffee shop. She's the GOAT.

As with most popular Gen-A terms, the means of transmission remains primarily memes. In the case of GOAT, there's a viral video of an anonymous man arguing with someone off-camera, defending someone anonymous by repeatedly yelling, face covered in sweat, eyes bulging, "That's why he's the GOAT! The GOAT!" No one knows the origin of that clip, nor does anyone care. All they care about is adding that clip to the end of their six-second short videos to establish someone's goatedness. It's reminiscent of a now canceled music artist using a sound bite from the movie Blades of Glory: "No one knows what it means, but it's provocative...It gets the people going!"

The term is probably more associated with videogame culture than it is with any other sub-culture. Every year, the Game Awards have a GOTY award, which stands for Game of the Year. Now, that award is yearly, so GOTY is a title that many games share with each other. Elden Ring is GOTY. So is God of War. Hades is also Game of the Year.

But what game is the GOAT?

Be careful, now. You don't want to be asking this question in a room full of gamers because that's how massacres happen. Everyone is extremely opinionated about which game is the GOAT, and most of them differ in their opinion.

The Witcher 3? Now, there would be some who call that game the GOAT. But then you'd have Playstation fanboys charging with the cries of Bloodborne, proclaiming it the greatest game of all time. Xbox fans will rush forth and rally to the cry of Halo being the GOAT. Then, the Nintendo fan base will come to defend their beloved Zelda games as the GOAT.

You'd be playing with live ammo if you were to casually ask a bunch of gamers this question. You're unlikely to be the victim, but the mere disagreement turned conflict you introduced could be considered premeditated.

There have been hilarious miscommunications based on the generational gap between people around the word GOAT. While shooting the movie Don't Look Up, everyone kept calling Meryl Streep GOAT. So, she eventually responded with, "Yeah, sure, just keep calling me an old goat." And then Jennifer Lawrence had to jump in and clarify that no one was actually calling her an old goat but a GOAT–The Greatest of All Time.

EXAMPLES

If you do something good for someone, and if that someone belongs to the Gen-Z/Gen-A group, they're probably going to respond with, "You did not just do that. On God, you're the GOAT."

If a teacher delays a test or gives the class an early leave, they're the GOAT. "Mr. Walter said that he wasn't going to teach us anything on account of working a shift at his meth lab. The guy's a GOAT."

If you like a particular show and if said show has earned a lot of critical acclaim, you can safely label it as the GOAT without a lot of people clawing at your throat. "Did you catch the last season of GOT? That show is literally the GOAT." If you did say that, though, I would have to suggest you watch The Penguin!

In the hierarchy of the Gen-A pyramid, GOATs are a step above sigmas because while there may be a lot of sigmas who can mog and mew like they mean it, there's only one GOAT. However, a term used so loosely is diluted in its meaning.

So, who's yours?

You know who's mine? There's this gag game series called the Goat Simulator where you play as a goat, and that's it. Well, that was it for the first couple of games, but ever since the games blew up, the latest Goat Simulator has everything from super-powers to the multiverse and complex storylines that rival the Avengers in terms of nuance.

That's my GOAT. The one in Goat Simulator. The original goat, of course.

EIGHT
GYATT
FOR WHEN ALL HYPERBOLE FAILS

IF NOT ANYTHING ELSE, it's a very explosive term. It comes out of nowhere, catching you by surprise. *GYATT!* And before you've had a chance to gather your senses following the sharp sound you didn't invite into your ear holes, the word's already been uttered. It's intensity diminishing into an ether you never wanted to be part of. It's akin to the sound of a car backfiring or a firecracker going off just behind you.

GYATT!

It hits you, and then before you've oriented yourself, it's gone.

Chronic internet users on Twitch, Reddit, TikTok, and X (formerly known as Twitter) have straight up shunned your garden variety exclamations in favor of terms such as BOMBOCLAT! and GYATT! The idea behind the all-capital nature of these words is that since you can't hear other people online, the loudest and most boisterous way to make your presence known is through several dozen exclamation marks and words written in uppercase. Old People Facebook is almost entirely filled with capslock ridiculousness, but this is different as it's intentional juxtaposition.

ORIGINS

The word's origins reflect its nature. It popped out of nowhere and then took over the internet overnight.

You can trace its origins to as far back as 2009 when the term Gyatt was used as an alternative for goddamn. However, the real credit goes to Nicki Minaj, creator of such fine musical masterpieces such as Anaconda, Super Bass, and Pound the Alarm. Side note: I once was in a work-related contest with my boss for the best karaoke performance of Super Bass.

Nicki Minaj, a female rap icon, used the term back in 2012 and then once again in 2014. Her tweets gained traction to the point that the term came to the forefront of the lexicon. She's the precursor for the term's later resurgence in 2021.

But in the summer of 2021, you had streamers like YourRage, Kai Cenat, and iShowSpeed (primarily black streamers) who used this term as part of their African American Vernacular English (AAVE) slang.

YourRage, a popular streamer, said, "Everybody used to say 'god damn' or 'golly,' but I said it weird. I'd always say 'gyatt,' I would never say 'god damn.' Chat realized that, and as a way of making fun of me in 2020, they started typing 'gyatt' to mock me."

In terms of evolution, the American linguist John McWhorter states that the term evolved from the word 'goddamn.' According to Kelly Wright, a research fellow in language sciences at Virginia Tech, GYATT emerges from Black Southern, Jamaican, and other communities of the African diaspora, therefore having its roots in the AAVE.

DEFINITION

Its rich history certainly contributes to its modern-day usage, with it being the primary catchphrase of streamers like Kai Cenat and iShowSpeed, who both have a very vivacious, loud, and boisterous online personality. They rely upon exclamations, hyperbole, and high energy behavior that resonates with their audience.

But when it comes to the meaning of the term, there's no denying that Gyatt is used to refer to a woman's posterior. When an attractive person passes by, those in the know yell Gyatt rather aggressively, directing the attention of others toward the object in question.

So, naturally, the exclamation becoming associated with derrieres, people started to come up with backronyms such as "Girl Your Ass Is Thick," or "Girl, You Ate That," or even the strangely unrelated and much sobering "Get Your Act Together."

With Gyatt, there's an even higher form of exaggeration, and that's the prefixing of levels with the term. For example, if you see a particularly good-looking woman, and her body is extremely curvy, she's not a level one or a level five, but she's a level ten Gyatt.

EXAMPLES

You don't always use Gyatt in a physical way. I mean, sure, that's the primary context, with an example being, "The minute that she walked by me in that dress, all I could think was GYATT!" but there are also non-physical contexts that you can use it in.

Humorous reactions are one. "My dog did a skibidi backflip off the couch. Gyatt! I didn't know she had it in her!"

You can be creative and intersperse this diverse word in everyday usage, such as, "That pizza delivery was so fast. GYATT! Dude must've flown here."

You may use it to express shock. "Gyatt! You finished Elden Ring already!?"

You can use it however you intend. A nonsense word that can mean everything and anything as long as you're using it on the internet amongst online friends. For example, "Don't be looking at me with your GYATT face."

That is how slang evolves. From a word that was used to express attraction and shock upon seeing a beautiful woman, the word Gyatt has become a versatile exclamation of awe and surprise.

But at its heart, it remains tied to the inanity of meme culture, proving that even the most niche terms can just explode into the mainstream when amplified by streamers and social media.

NINE
LETS MELT SOME MINDS TOGETHER
YOUR REVIEW = BRAIN FOOD FOR THE MASSES

A good book is the true magic potion, and the best magic happens when you share it.

TOTALLY NOT SOCRATES

IF YOU'VE FLIPPED through these pages and found yourself laughing, questioning reality, or maybe just squinting a little harder at the ceiling fan, then you're already part of something bigger.

WHY SHOULD YOU BOTHER?

I know what you're thinking: "Why me?" Well, reviews aren't just words; they're signposts for other wandering minds. Your review might be the very spark that nudges someone into discovering this masterpiece.

Let's break it down:

- It takes about 60 seconds. That's less time than it takes to figure out why your phone is upside down.
- It's free.
- It makes a difference. Not just for the book, but for all the future Brainrots out there looking for something to ignite their gray matter.

READY TO MELT MINDS?

TEN

ISHOWSPEED AND KAI CENAT
THE ARCHITECTS OF GEN-A SLANG

ANY MENTION of Gen-A slang would be incomplete without the two online sensations who have contributed most to it. Go to Wikipedia for most of the entries in this book, and in their origins section you shall find Kai Cenat or iShowSpeed mentioned.

In the Gen-Z vernacular book that I wrote some years ago, I mentioned the pioneers of internet pop culture, such as PewDiePie and Smosh, people who belonged to the millennial age group and had a lot of contributions toward Gen-Z slang.

As baffling as it is to believe, we are in the next cycle already. Now, these two Gen-Z content creators are contributing heartily toward Gen-A slang, and so it is the circle of life.

It goes beyond just slang, though. These two streamers, and all their associated acts such as Fanum and Adin Ross, have been at the forefront of transforming the online content space, standing upon the shoulders of giants such as Jacksepticeye, Markiplier, and PewDiePie. They're figures who started the whole streaming sub-culture. They've since then passed the baton to these new kids on the block while themselves soft-retiring and doing things that they like.

Do you know what PewDiePie is doing these days? The thirty-four-year-old former most-subscribed YouTuber has officially stopped making his quintessential videos and now lives in Japan with his wife and one-year-old son, making mellower Japanese vlogs and quite sober commentary videos. Because apparently, that's what you do after you've been at the top of your game for more than a decade. On the internet, a decade is more like a century.

Another example is Joji. You are truly one of God's blessed people if you haven't watched a Filthy Frank video. Please stay blessed and stay away from those videos because not only are they the most politically incorrect form of content out there, but they're also immensely gross. I'm not even going to go into it. But I will tell you that Joji, the guy behind Filthy Frank and Pink Guy, hung up his costumes and cowls and has since then gone into a more serious direction. Hilariously enough, we, the millennials, know him for his depraved online presence. The Gen-Z and Gen-A, who completely skipped out on the early 2010s (when Filthy Frank was in his prime), only knew him from his heartfelt music. Yeah. The guy did a 180-degree pivot and now makes highly successful music.

In the wake of the absence of all the fathers of online culture, you've got the newcomers picking up the baton and taking things up a notch. Both of them have a very similar content creation style. Instead of specializing in a specific niche, they go across the board. They play games, invite guests over, make travel vlogs, comment on internet happenings such as YouTube drama, which is a gold mine for content, and collaborate with each other. When all else fails, cause intentional controversy™.

And you might be wondering who's watching these kids jumping over sports cars and getting arrested for making fake phone calls to police officers. Who is the demographic enjoying this highly exaggerated, somewhat sexually charged, extremely hyperactive content when all the adults are off doing their jobs, and all the older teens and younger adults are busy with the motions of school and college life, interning, and scrambling to land their first jobs?

Kids.

That's who.

The millions of viewers who spend actual money to pay for subscriptions and gifts are children in the age range of 9 to 15. The most susceptible and vulnerable minds are viewing the shenanigans of these content creators. These kids, in a bid to stay online for as long as their content creators remain online, suffer from brainrot; they speak in the way that iShowSpeed, Kai Cenat, Adin Ross, Fanum, et al. speak and act.

On the one hand, you've got these streamers meeting some of the biggest names of various industries–Ronaldo, Jordan Peterson, Nicki Minaj, Messi, Ice Spice, Doja Cat, Tyla, and John Cena to name a few–and are being propelled to mainstream fame and acknowledgment. On the other, they're unwittingly promoting boisterous behavior.

iShowSpeed has a catchphrase which is not exactly a word but a series of aggressive barks. It's an extremely loud sound that serves to disconcert. The same is true for Kai Cenat and his array of guttural exclamatory sounds.

What happens when you've got two of the biggest names in streaming creating unhealthy amounts of noise?

It reaches millions of impressionable minds trying to mimic their favorite streamers in real life, too much of which ends with the aforementioned brainrot.

To leave it on an open-ended note, the presence of such larger-than-life streamers is a testament to the power of platforms like TikTok and YouTube, but it is also a perpetrator of behavior that goes beyond just slang.

ELEVEN

LOOKSMAXXING
MAXING YOUR APPEARANCE STATS AND IGNORING THE REST

DO you remember your teenage years? I think that most of us can remember explicit details from our teenage years, especially when it comes to being a little insecure about our looks. An acne blossom of insecurity, basking in the limelight of pubescent cheeks. Braces. Facial and body hair taking root.

Puberty is nothing short of a nightmare. It's every visceral thing happening to you at the same time, hormones raging, werewolf transformations happening under the bleachers, and hot vampires forced to repeat the same grades over and over again in different cities so that no one grows suspicious.

There's a chance that I've forgotten my own teenage years and am now remembering the Twilight movies instead. Pay me no heed. My skin does not shine bright like diamonds. I could never be Edward Cullen even if I tried.

See what I did there? I envied Robert Pattinson and found myself coming up short in terms of the looks and personality department because I'm just regular old me and Rob Pat is one of the most popular movie stars of this era. He completely redefined himself after the Twilight series, and went on to do award-winning roles such as the Batman and that time-traveling soldier dude in Christopher Nolan's Tenet.

Now, I'm a relatively well-adjusted adult and can move beyond my envy. But what happens when young, impressionable teenagers undergo a brand of envy that rears its head right along the time when they're growing up?

That's when these kids take things into their own hands and ascribe to the belief system of looksmaxxing. Because in the age of PowerBI and customizable character building menus, why shouldn't your looks also boil down to a series of adjustable 'metrics.'

If you can max out your physical attractiveness by fine-tuning your attributes, then you can achieve social, financial, and even romantic success. At least that's the idea behind looksmaxxing.

And would you be surprised that this viral phenomenon that's implemented both ironically and unironically gained traction on incel forums to begin with?

ORIGINS

Incels, also known as involuntary celibates on account of no one's going to date them because of their reprehensible personality and lack of hygiene, often live in delusion. They think that the reason why prospective partners won't talk to them and society won't treat them with seriousness is because it's society who's at fault, not themselves.

That girl didn't seem interested in your fifteen-minute monologue on Andrew Tate's matrix-breaking plan? Clearly, she's a part of the matrix and was sent to distract you. It has nothing to do with the fact that you're spewing misogynistic propaganda uttered by one of the most deplorable online personalities. Nope. It's the girl who's at fault here.

You'll find limitless examples online, where incels do not take accountability for their attitude, personality, and behavior, and instead blame the world at large for not understanding them.

Big yikes.

As unhinged as it all sounds, that's where looksmaxxing originated from. On incel forums such as Lookism, PUAhate, and Sluthate in the early 2010s where a congress of incels unanimously decided that if you're not succeeding in attaining a partner, it's because your looks are not maxed out yet. To improve their sexual market value, these incels proposed extreme measures, believing that physical attractiveness alone was the key to success with women.

The term leaked into mainstream culture by the 2020s, and now you've got TikTok drawing the attention of younger audiences towards an unhealthy phenomenon created by incels.

The concept is tied to self-esteem issues, as young people are encouraged to evaluate themselves harshly and obsess over their perceived physical flaws. Looksmaxxing promotes an unhealthy fixation on appearance to achieve a perfect look that will result in romantic success.

DEFINITION

At its core, the term refers to the process of maximizing your looks through one of two main avenues–softmaxxing and hardmaxxing.

Softmaxxing is a milder form of maximizing your looks and involves basic hygiene and body care routines in order to look and feel better. To quote reddit:

Step 1: Be attractive

Step 2: Don't be unattractive

Some of these practices are harmless and in fact beneficial for you, such as bridging the mountainous gaps previously formed by youth and bacteria with Retin-A, going to the gym, taking a shower, brushing your teeth, or perhaps getting a new haircut.

But that's just the tip of the iceberg because you're still within the realm of softmaxxing. Meaning you're not really serious about looking good.

So, you take things up a notch and start exercise routines that alter your facial and body structure. Welcome to hardmaxxing, where surgeries, mewing (exercises designed to reshape your jawline), bone smashing (yes, literally hitting your face to try and alter its structure), limb lengthening surgery, and implants are the go-to method to alter your appearance in a way that it's permanent or long-lasting.

The idea behind looksmaxxing is to look like Patrick Bateman from American Psycho, who himself had a meticulous daily routine. I mean, are we forgetting the fact that Patrick Bateman was a murderous psychopath who displayed psychopathic tendencies throughout the movie? But these Gen-A kids don't care about that. They care about acquiring the Patrick Bateman look with the hunter eyes, strong jawline, and hollow cheeks—features that supposedly signal masculinity and dominance.

Some men max out their physical appearance and refer to themselves as being Y-pilled, a spin on the 'red-pilled' ideology from the Matrix movies. While red-pilled refers to awakening to harsh truths about society, being Y-pilled means you embrace hyper-masculinity so that your physical dominance over others increases your status and attractiveness.

EXAMPLES

I feel we're in a pretty dark corner of the internet, discussing something that should be taboo, but that's Gen-A slang for you. In some cases, such as this one, it does not care that terms like looksmaxxing and brainrot signify a deeper psychological problem and only cares to use these terms in a humorous capacity.

"I've been looksmaxxing lately, hitting the gym, fixing my skincare routine, and mewing on the daily. It's all about becoming a sigma rizzler" is a sentence that seems straight out of a fever dream but is probably quite often used by Gen-A folk, and as bizarre as it sounds, it's a sentence that conveys a lot of meaning. One that perhaps highlights the severity of self-esteem issues that the younger generation faces in the wake of this constant need to look your best for people online.

TWELVE

MEWING FOR A BETTER JAWLINE

WHEN DR. JOHN MEW and Dr. Mike Mew, two British orthodontists, came up with the technique of pressing your tongue against the roof of your mouth to improve your jawline aesthetics over time, I'm pretty certain they did not anticipate their do-it-yourself oral posture training technique's name would become a Gen-A slang term.

ORIGINS

But that's what happened.

The concept of mewing was created by Dr. Mike Mew as a part of his broader orthotropic approach aimed at guiding facial development, especially in children and teens. You hold your tongue in a specific posture and it's supposed to lead to sharper jawlines and more defined cheekbones by altering your literal bone structure. While some of these claims are pseudoscientific, they have not deterred Gen-A from adopting this technique and putting it in their looksmaxxing toolkit to transform themselves into young versions of Patrick Bateman.

I have a feeling we're still in that dark place of the internet, Ray.

And since we're already here, we might as well discuss the consequences of TikToks that aren't backed by a lot of research. In the short-form, short attention span era of the internet that the Gen-A is growing up in, it's no longer trendy to look something up and confirm if it's actually true or not. If there's a big enough influencer behind the information, it must be true. They couldn't possibly be putting their reputation on the line, could they?

By 2023, the term mewing evolved beyond its original purpose and morphed into a punchline, a gesture used in classrooms! Gen-A teens began mewing to signal that they were too busy looksmaxxing to answer questions or participate because their tongues were placed against the roof of their mouths. They used this gesture as a way to avoid conversations and classroom participation.

Teachers realized that their students were shushing each other with their fingers and tracing their jawlines to signify that they were mewing and couldn't speak. This passive form of defiance has since then become a source of frustration for educators, as not only does it disrupt the classroom environment, but it's also perceived as disrespectful.

DEFINITION

Much of both Gen-Z and Gen-A slang has to do with gestures. The iconic 'ice in my veins' gesture that the Gen-Z popularized is an example of that. Dabbing is yet another one. You'll see a trend where the gestures have grown smaller and more subtle in terms of what they mean. People aren't doing entire Fortnite dances to convey what they're doing anymore. They're just running their finger along their jawline to indicate that they're mewing.

Mewing and looksmaxxing are part of a larger problem called lookism on the internet, a phenomenon perpetrated by incels wherein they claim that it's all about looks. Their claim is that the difference between flirting and harassment is not in the way that you flirt, but in the way that you look. If you're a handsome person, any flirting that you do will be perceived as positive, but if you're not gifted in the looks department, any flirting that you do will be perceived as harassment.

While it is objectively flawed, it hasn't stopped this premise from propagating into other aspects of Gen-A slang, such as mogging, which is a term that describes one person dominating the other based on how physically attractive they look, and derogative remarks towards women that ironically tend to pigeonhole them as superficial and only caring about a person's appearance.

You see the irony, right? The incels are the ones insecure about their appearance and are projecting that insecurity onto others, furthering their own misogyny.

It has been of no help that manosphere content creators such as Andrew Tate have substantiated these claims with groundless statements of their own, claiming that women can literally smell if you're a beta or an alpha.

Rule of thumb—if someone's been arrested and imprisoned on several harassment charges, has had a history of running illegal businesses involving trafficking and coercion, and often picks fights with climate activists, that's not the person you should be following for advice.

EXAMPLES

As serious as the subject matter is, with Gen-A, nothing remains serious for long. They turn everything into a meme, and that meme goes viral. Before you've had the opportunity for some serious discourse on the matter, it all devolves into laughter and hilarity.

Someone using the phrase mewing might do it to disrupt the environment in a classroom by stating loudly, "Hey, stop asking me questions, skibidi! I'm busy mewing!"

Teens might use it to reference physical improvement such as by saying, "I've been mewing for six months, and now my jawline is starting to look more sigma."

It can also be used light-heartedly, such as, "The cat's been mewing so much that it's got a sharper jawline than I do."

As it continues to evolve, mewing is an example of how niche practices (even if they're pseudoscientific medical practices) can be repurposed into slang and social behavior that can shape online and offline interactions as well as your jawline.

THIRTEEN

THE REPLY-ALL INCIDENT

From: bobj@thehipcompany.com

To: departmentoflabor@usdoj.gov

Cc: peers@thehipcompany.com, richardcashmore@thehipcompany.com, blakebalderdash@thehipcompany.com

Fwd: Re: Celebrate wins! Pizza party this Friday at 6pm

To whom it may concern,

I think we need to talk. See the forwarded e-mail from our CEO. Accidental reply-all.

Signed,
Bob

BLAKE!

How'd that pizza party go? Glad I missed it. The last time we had one of these those dinosaurs of people approached me to ask about raises or bonuses. Like, HELLO? This schmuck was saying he'd rather have a raise than pizza. I mean, we're feeding you! How much more family can we be? I had to put in my noise-canceling earbuds and pretend to take a call to get out of there. I'll bet the Gen-A were busting out Fortnite emote moves to the infectious rhythm of Travis Scott or Playboi Carti.

How's it hanging at the fifth floor? I bet you can't wait till your promotion to VP next year. If you get that promotion, that is. Jennie's been working overtime (if you know what I mean) to make sure that I keep her in my good books. Looks like you've got your competition cut out for you for that sweet seventh floor corner office, eh? Tell you what, if you keep doing the Lord's (that's me) work, you'll probably end up in my office one day. On second thought, probably not, but I don't want to stop you from dreaming.

Hey, listen. Thanks. Like, for the whole GYATT thing, man. I mean it. It was your idea, wasn't it? I figured it was, because if there's anyone who hates those saggy ass fogies moseying about the corridors as much as me, it's you. Head of legal tells me this is fucking genius, my guy.

She says that this is the perfect indirect option strategy we could have deployed. The last thing we needed was direct action, because let's face it, if you or me or anyone else were even a teensy bit blunt about our preferences in our workforce's age, we'd have been hit with a class action lawsuit like were piñatas at Miguel's daughter's quinceañera. Speaking of which, remind me to never eat the dip at Miguel's house. It tasted like what comes out in the bathroom after you eat the dip. These diversity hires, I tell ya.

Anyways, you're a beautiful bastard for coming up with this GYATT initiative. This is the best thing that you could have pulled. Get a load of these fogies trailing down the hall like they're extras in a nursing home commercial. Soon, my friend, they'll be gone with the wind. And I most certainly won't miss their wind. Especially Phyllis's. It's as if the woman is exclusively gas-propelled. And you can't say anything, because if you say something, it means that you're admitting that you're acknowledging that she's ripped a fat one.

Imagine it. No more Phyllis. No more Bob. No more of the zombies in the accounting section. That whole floor smells like mothballs, formaldehyde, and dead dreams. I'd much rather have it smell of that passionfruit vape flavor that the new kid's always puffing in the break-room. Now that's the kind of cojones I need around here. Kid's got like half a dozen HR warnings, but does that stop him from ripping those fat clouds? He calls himself Skizzy. Skizzy installed Fortnite on my work computer yesterday so we could get an office LAN party going. That's more of what I want, Blake.

· · ·

Not Phyllis with her weather forecast conversations. If I find her one more time at the water cooler talking about low pressure systems, I'm going to french kiss the business end of a shotgun. No more of her tupperware lunches that look and smell like she got a serving of sloppy gruel from Oliver Twist. Please sir, can I have some more? Not to mention Bob, the big lumbering idiot from QA, always talking about "back in my day", "growing up with respect for elders", and his war stories about 'Nam. I have it on good authority Bob was enjoying a prolonged vacation in Canada during the Vietnam war. Which is why this GYATT thing is perfect. They don't understand it, they don't want to understand it, and that's exactly what we're banking on. The more Gen-A slang we throw in the mix, the more alienated they're going to feel, and before you know, out they go. Don't let the door hit ya where God split ya. Remember that? We used to say that a lot. The best part about their quitting would be that it's going to be voluntary, saving us from paying out severances, pensions, and throwing those asinine retirement parties with those godawful sheet cakes they all love.

We're on the right track, I'm telling you. I attended one of those mandatory meetings and some of the older members of our workforce were sitting there drooling from their faces, looking at each other as if the meeting was in Greek. Meanwhile, I was like, finally someone's speaking my language. I've been edging since before it was cool, bro. Maybe we'll have more of those meetings. Something like a mandatory TikTok day, where you can only speak in trendy catchphrases, or a Gen-A glossary pop-quiz. If anyone doesn't know the difference between skibidi and sigma, they're probably a better fit for a retirement village than this office. A better fit for Ohio, more like. The second these old dogs who can't be taught new tricks leave, this whole place gets a facelift. We'll have Fortnite dance-offs, mewing competitions the winner of which will be labelled Mogchamp of the Month, and performance reports that will be judged by who's the most sigma. Imagine it, Blake. A meme-literate workforce that's fun to be around.

Anyway, keep up God's work. I'm counting on you to push the GYATT initiative even further, even if Jennifer might be pushing herself into that VP office first. It's a dog-eat-dog world out there, and only the sharpest dog gets to sit at the top.

Catch you later,

Bossman

FOURTEEN
MOGGING
EMBODYING PERFECTION

WHAT DO you get when you mew for a year straight and go hard on looksmaxxing? Well, you achieve your goal of becoming the fittest and sexiest, and therefore, have turned yourself into the alpha male of the group, aka, AMOG. Now, when you walk, people notice. When you enter a room, heads turn in your direction in sheer awe. That's what you get when you put in the work and put in the hours. You become a mogchamp, a looksmaxxing goat, a mewing sigma worthy of all the GYATT people exclaim when they look at your hunter's eyes, at your square jaw, at your ripped muscles, and your domineering gait.

A mogger has all the positive aura in the world, is free from the weak burdens and shackles of lesser men such as brainrot, is always the main character of the story no matter which story it is, and when he does something, he straight up cooks, and in doing so, dominates everyone.

Or so he thinks.

That's the problem with the term and its meaning.

You see, there's a fine difference between being a sigma and thinking that you're the sigma.

ORIGINS

The term originates from the cesspool of incel and far-right behavior, 4chan, where a post in 2016 describes a 7-foot-tall bodybuilder who is so muscular and powerful that he shall mog them all. In the same sense as Sauron's one ring rules them all. Eight years since the term got coined, the meaning remains the same, and has not been able to shed its incel culture nature.

It's peak self-conceited behavior that evokes comparison and trying to assess who's more handsome than the other.

A truly dominating person does not keep a stat sheet of all the attributes in which he dominates others. A mogger, on the other hand, has a diverse array of stats in which he mogs others. For example, height-mogging is when you're taller than someone else. Jaw-mogging is when your jawline is sharper than your peers. Hairmogging occurs when you've got a full head of luscious hair that outshines and outgrows that of a balding individual. And then you have the vainest of them all, agemogging, which is when a younger person flexes being younger and more attractive than an older person.

DEFINITION

In lookism (the umbrella slang term referring to prejudice and discrimination towards people's physical appearance), mogging means asserting your dominance over other men in the hope that you will impress more women. The word comes from pickup artist communities that are preoccupied with tricks and schemes to attract women as opposed to simply going up and talking to them. This sub-culture has insidiously misogynistic views of women and thinks of them as objects or lesser beings who are attracted to superficial aspects of one's person.

It's such an unhealthy echo chamber that no one questions their outdated and condescending views, and instead furthers each other's misconception that attractive people live life on easy mode simply because they earn more respect from their peers and women alike.

But then you have intellectuals within this sub-culture who take mogging to another level and fuse it with intelligence, money, and clothes. As a result, you have smartmogging, where you flex your IQ online and establish your intelligence over other people, moneymogging, where you boast your wealth in the face of someone who's not as rich as you are, and dressmogging, where you rub it in someone's face that they're not as well-dressed as you are.

This sick spiral goes even deeper, and when meme culture picked it up, they just went crazy with it, implying that moggers will do anything to get their hands on some protein (semen being one of those sources) and creatine.

If you find yourself scrolling too far down social media, you're bound to come across influencers promoting gym culture to the younger generation, all in the name of performative, comparative gains instead of actual self-improvement.

Scroll even further down, and you will come across influencers like the Liver King promoting straight-up dangerous activities like eating raw liver to give yourself the true, masculine alpha form that your ancestors have. A year or so ago, the Liver King was debunked and publicly humiliated after it was leaked that this 'natural' physique that he claimed he had was a result of steroids and hormones.

EXAMPLES

Its more grievous aspects aside, the term retains its rank as one of the most favorite Gen-A slang terms and is used in all sorts of contexts, most of them being light-hearted and a majority of them centered around fitness and self-improvement.

If a friend in a group has a shorter height than the rest, they might say something along the lines of, "I got mogged hard by everyone in the group photo. I'm not fine being a short king."

Short king is another tangential slang, a term of endearment and encouragement for those whose heights are shorter than 5'8". Even if they're short, they're still a king.

In most competitive multiplayer games like Valorant and Over-watch (games that are exceedingly popular amongst the Gen-A and make me miss the good old days of Counter Strike and Quake), one guy usually carries the rest of the team, and when they do, their team says, "ShortKing420 mogged hard. Did you see his kill streak? Total sigma."

If a woman dresses better than everyone else, she no longer slays or kills. She mogs. More specifically, her outfit mogs all the other dresses.

Here's a little easter egg for you. There are actually two terms that go by MOG. One is the looksmaxxing related use that we've discussed at length, and the other one stands for Man of God, Gen-A's version of implying someone is deeply religious and spiritual. It's a very niche phrase popular within Christian circles on the internet, showing the duality of slang and how secular slang can also be used by a non-secular audience.

So whether you're in the mood for some jawline mogging or becoming a mog by letting the secrets of the universe unfold unto your deep spirit, make sure that you mog in moderation and that the designated driver does not mog at all. Because that's how you end up in Ohio.

And trust me, you do not want to go to Ohio.

FIFTEEN
ONLY IN OHIO

THE MERE MENTION of Ohio will cast a shadow of fear upon the faces of Gen-A, who are all in on the secret that if there is hell on this earth, it is Ohio. Forget Florida. It's now Ohio that is the den of all things eerie and out of the ordinary. It's no longer this boring Midwestern state known for its cornfields and Cleveland.

Oh, no, sir. It's a bizarre carnival of all things odd. Urban legends roam in the wastelands of this strange land that is worse than any liminal space you've known all your life. Backrooms are easy mode compared to Ohio. Because guess what? You cannot escape Ohio.

You may find yourself whisked to Ohio like you're Dorothy, but that's where the comparison stops. This ain't Oz. This is the land of absurdity, a land with people tweaking on Grimace Shakes, odd life forms wearing the guise of humans torturing you with their sick games that make Jigsaw from SAW shiver in fear. They will trap you in the basement of their boring middle-of-nowhere suburban house and ask you bizarre riddles in a bid to drive you insane.

Suppose, by some longshot, that you actually do make it out of that basement and run for your life, what happens when you reach the state's border?

You've got Ohio Final Boss, Satoyu, waiting there for you. He's the most powerful form of menace out there, and unhinged in a way that is only possible in Ohio. He rules this storm-struck wasteland, the devourer of all things at the end of the void.

This world full of monsters, mayhem, and melancholy is home to a multitude of memes and popular phraseology, all of which have something to do with Ohio.

You have been warned.

Stephen King couldn't conjure up a scarier state if he tried.

ORIGINS

A 2016 Tumblr post featured a broken bus stop with a sign that read, "Ohio will be terminated." Naturally, the meme caught fire and left people wondering what Ohio did to deserve such a fate. As it spread across other platforms, the concept of this liminal version of Ohio caught on, a world that's cursed and is soon to be eliminated. Abandoned parking lots. Flickering lights. Storm clouds gathering and roaring on the horizon. Darkness all around. This is Ohio.

2019 saw Ohio memes morphing into another meme called "Wait, it's Ohio? Always has been," which sort of implies that the entire world is basically Ohio.

Enter the post-Covidian era, and before you knew it, in 2022, people were fully embracing the psychological fear-fest that was Ohio, with dark shadowy figures moving around in hallways and empty streets, skibidi toilet heads haunting unsuspecting people in the suburban hellscape, and your worse nightmares materializing in front of your eyes in this Gen-A equivalent of Dante's Inferno.

These memes often had captions like "Can't even sleep in Ohio" on account of all the horrors lurking around the corners. "Can't have peace in Ohio" because of all the elements of terror and torture aplenty in this seemingly innocuous state that is, in reality, the breeding ground of all things evil.

And if you see something that defies all explanation, you just say, "Only in Ohio." Because that's where all the weird stuff happens.

As if that was not enough, rapper Lil B's song "Swag Like Ohio" served as the perfect surreal soundtrack to all the inexplicable phenomena happening in Ohio.

DEFINITION

How do you define the undefinable chasm beyond the known universe? Is there a word for the abyss? Yes, it's Ohio. Ohio represents the absurdist, dystopian, post-apocalyptic version of America where each survivor lives for himself and nothing makes sense and everything is out of control.

Is the panic setting in?

Good. Now, you know that you have to avoid Ohio or being labeled as Ohio at all costs.

It doesn't matter that Lebron hailed from Akron, Ohio. It does not matter that the Rock and Roll Hall of Fame is located in Ohio. It certainly does not mean anything that modern aviation, as we know it, originated from Ohio.

Because three or four good things cannot possibly outweigh the nastiness, the dread, the dystopia that is Ohio. It's a state of mind unlike the Empire State of Mind because this state of mind represents brainrot at its finest. It's after a person has guzzled two whole liters of Grimace Shake (a limited edition purple-colored shake released by McDonalds) and is lying on the side-walk convulsing with purple froth coming out of their mouth.

People have made videos—both animated and real—on TikTok about trying to survive in Ohio's horrors. Giant skeletal figures prowl through the neighborhood. Spectral red eyes peer from behind the veil of perpetual darkness, marking you as their prey.

It's everything bad, everything cringe, everything dreadful, all summed up in one word.

This capitalistic wasteland of chaos, this devastating ode to all things creepypasta—Ohio.

EXAMPLES

This slang is so rich that it's got its own little bubble of specific phrases. There's Ohio Final Boss, a representation of a demonically powerful being that prowls this wasteland. There's also Ohio Queen, who, in the anime vein of Ohio Final Boss, is another archetypal character that is found in Ohio.

Then you've got your garden variety phraseology such as "Can't even 'XYZ' in Ohio," where users show footage of frightening things happening in their vicinity. Things that are preventing them from, say, ordering a pizza, walking their dog, or going to Walmart.

Another level deeper in this rabbit hole, you'll figure out that Ohio is an outlandish place where all eerie and paranormal things happen exclusively. They do not occur in Wisconsin, nor in New Jersey, and most certainly not in California. If something's off-kilter, it happens "only in Ohio."

And lastly, to completely sum up the existential dread that is Ohio, there's a phrase that goes, "It's all Ohio? Always has been," which refers to the fact that you, wherever you are, have always been in Ohio. That Ohio secretly dominates the entire universe to the point that any place, any time, anywhere is part of Ohio. And knowing this makes you one of the rare few who have just discovered the maddening truth of the matter.

Do take all of this with massive grains of salt because it's just Gen-A humor, and at the end of the day, Ohio only means something bad, strange, weird, cringe, or dumb.

Or does it?

SIXTEEN

POOKIE
GEN-A'S TERM OF ENDEARMENT

THE EVOLUTION of terms of endearment over the past century has been something of a marvel to behold. Most of us have grown alongside it. We remember our parents referring to each other as sugar, honey, honeybuns, sweetie cakes, or even babe. And that's what we took forward. In the late 20th and early 21st century, terms of endearment still retained their original endearing familiarity mixed with a little bit of formality. Your significant other was your babe, or baby.

ORIGINS

But then, the 2010s rolled around, and we suddenly decided that it was no longer cool to call them babe. Bae would have to suffice, even though bae is the official Danish word for feces. But the word stuck, and the world forgot that bae, the word denoting the love of your life, also stood for poop in Danish.

It's the same with Pookie. I mean, Gen-A's intents might be sincere with this cute word, but it means fart. In the official entry on Urban Dictionary, pookie is gas that travels from your butt to the front of your crotch. I'm serious. Look it up.

But that has not stopped Gen-A from using this term for their significant other, best friend, or anyone that they want to serenade with this label of endearment.

On a serious note, the term has been around as a nickname as far back as the 1930s, and it spread around the United States in the 60s as a term for your loved one. However, it became popular in the 2020s when TikTok got a hold of it, and JayRScotty, known for Two Pretty Best Friends, started to call her viewers pookie.

It's understated how viral that term became. Official handles of Netflix use the term now to refer to their fans, among thousands of other official accounts on social media trying to keep up with the latest slang to connect with their consumers. Netflix does a thing on their WhatsApp channel called Pookie Roll Call, taking screenshots of people who want to be featured on the channel and posting it with some tongue-in-cheek zinger like "I can't get enough of my pookies!"

Dude, you should see a gastroenterologist if you can't get enough of your pookies.

With TikTok, you give them an inch, and they'll run with it. Now you've got variations of Pookie such as Pookie Wookie, Pookie Sweetie, and Pookie Bear.

It's harmless, it's adorable, and it's candid. Gen-A, like Gen-Z before them, are quite candid and frank in terms of making friends or partners. And they're more than frank when it comes to giving their partners loving titles. You may hear a girl call her boyfriend, 'My Batman' and you might think that this guy looks nothing like Bruce Wayne, but that doesn't matter, because to that girl, the guy represents Batman, her dark knight and ever vigilant protector.

MEANING

Pookie is inner-circle speak. Unlike the Freemason's handshake, it's not so secretive nor is gatekept that much. It's just a fine distinction. You're either someone's pookie or you're not. And if you are, good for you, because that means that your friend or partner—the one who calls you by that name—feels safe around you. It means that they love you enough to share this silly nickname with you. It means that they hold you to a standard of comfortable informality where you can refer to them as pookie and they'll love it back.

Pookie stands for someone who is cute. Someone who knows how to cheer you up on a sad day. Your pookie is someone who gets you boba tea without you even asking. At the end of the day, you'd rather spend time with your pookie than with anyone else because your pookie truly gets you.

They love you.

EXAMPLES

The term is both platonic and non-platonic, depending upon its use.

You could refer to your best friend as pookie, and you'd be using it in a platonic capacity. "She's my pookie; I don't go anywhere without her."

You could use it romantically, such as, "Me and my boyfriend call each other pookie, because that's where we're at."

There is a distinct set of people stuck in the friend zone who use this term with their crush on purpose so that they may see them as more than a friend. Because, while it is perfectly usable as a platonic term for your friend, the heavy implication behind the word is a romantic one. So, if you've got your crush failing to notice you, or has kept you in the friend zone for too long, calling them pookie might clear things up or end them altogether.

Use at your own discretion.

This is probably the best place to mention that online romantic relationships have evolved to the point that there are now ready-made reels, videos, and memes on social media that you can share with your partner in real-time and in quick succession. It's a new and rapid kind of love, one that's marked by memes and absurd videos that convey your unique love to your partner. It's like when you're on the toilet, browsing TikTok, and you come across a meme and you share it with your partner (who's probably not in the bathroom with you while you're going number 2) to let them know that you're thinking of them, even when heeding the call of nature.

The next time you see a sad-eyed cat meme with a caption, "Send this to your pookie if you're missing her," don't think—just share. You'll both be happier for it.

SEVENTEEN
RIZZLER ON THE ROOF

WHILE WRITING THIS BOOK, there was a point where I wondered if this slang warranted an entire book written around it. And then I looked at Oxford University Press's 2023 word of the year.

Can you guess what that word is?

Rizz.

It's impossible to dismiss the Oxford Dictionary as a gag book, because it is a literal encyclopedia of all known English words. And now, that encyclopedia includes all the terms that I've shared in this book so far.

In 2023, the global population seemed to be using one Gen-A slang word more than the rest. A word that became so popular that it became hard to ignore and earned its badge the way Goblin Mode earned its Word of the Year badge for 2022, and Vax earned the title for 2021.

So where does it come from, this remarkable, forever-in-the-annals-of-history word, and what does it mean?

Rizz—also known as Unspoken Rizz, is a term that is used to refer to the innate ability of a charismatic man to attract a partner without trying. This effortless charisma is dubbed as rizz, a shortening of the word charisma by only using the middle syllable of the word. Much like you use the word fridge for refrigerator, you use rizz for charisma.

ORIGINS

Remember Kai Cenat? Yep. He is heavily featured in the origins of this word. Kai Cenat, Silky, and Duke Dennis popularized this term in the middle of 2021, but as for the actual term, it originated in New York City slang a little bit earlier.

Kai Cenat has been using this word during his live streams and would share his insights on how you could possess rizz, going into sophisticated detail about W Rizz and L Rizz, which, respectively, is rizz that wins you a girl and rizz that loses you a potential mate, respectively.

The history behind this is a little silly. During the pandemic, live e-dates became a thing. Naturally, the two most chronically online streamers also jumped aboard the bandwagon and started to do these live e-dates. Silky and Kai Cenat watched each other talk to girls and then reacted to their conversations and overall performance, rating it on the metric of rizz.

For a couple years now, these casual, streamer-oriented dating shows have become more popular and common, where TikTokers, YouTubers, Twitch Streamers, internet celebs, and comedians host dating shows and give commentary on each other's flirting abilities.

After Kai Cenat's popularization of the term, video montages of Kai Cenat's best rizz moments started to surface on YouTube, and given his massive following, it was only a matter of time before this term entered the mainstream.

Similarly, Duke Dennis posted a tweet where he dubbed flirting with one's eyes as a skill in the repertoire of unspoken rizz.

In April 2022, this term was seen en masse on TikTok in a new format of videos called Rizz TikToks or RizzToks, where influencers would flirt with women and gauge their own rizz. If they succeeded, they flexed their abilities, and if they failed, well, it made for a hilarious video anyway.

This colloquial noun is used to denote the characteristic possessed by a charismatic man. When used as a verb, it's what a rizzler does to attract someone. This is also called rizzing someone up.

Since 2021, other variations of the word have developed, including Rizz God, Ohio Rizzler, Walt Rizzney, Rizzard of Oz, Edward Rizzlerhands, and Rizz Al Ghul (a reference to Batman's teacher). If it's a female in question, you can refer to her as Queen Erizzabeth.

DEFINITION

Rizz is basically game. If you've got game, then you've got rizz. It's just that no one actually uses the term game for charisma anymore. No longer do we define flirting by the ability to neg; no longer do we follow *The Game*, by Neil Strauss.

As for its meaning, it's not just about attracting another person. The term rizz, much like its parent term charisma, encompasses the way you talk, look, act, behave, and interact with other people.

There's a certain smoothness to someone with rizz, whether they're charming a room full of strangers or subtly flirting with a beautiful woman. People possessing rizz are often seen as extroverted because, go figure, it takes a lot of confidence and extroversion to go up to someone and talk to them.

However, there's another subtler type of rizz out there called quiet rizz. This is when you're an introvert—but secretly a sigma who cooks on the daily—and instead of being the first one to interact, you let your quiet aura of confidence and sex appeal do the talking for you. In these cases, the girl—or the person being rizzed—approaches the quiet rizzler instead.

There's also something known as rizzing someone up. It's when you're at a bar, and someone starts to chat with you. They're not just flirting; they're going the whole nine yards—touching your hand casually, buying you a drink, and being effortless in the way they talk, laugh, listen, and stay engaged. When you follow through with all of your charisma, you're said to be rizzing someone up. It's when you go all in and flirt hard.

There is a distinct line between rizzing someone up and straight-up harassing them. You gauge the other person's interest in you, and if they show an interest, you continue rizzing, but if it feels like they don't want to be a part of this interaction, then you respectfully back off. You take the L. You acknowledge your L Rizz. But you back off nevertheless because rizz isn't something that should be unwelcome. It can be unsolicited—as sometimes flirting is—but it should never make the other person uncomfortable. That's the hard line.

Someone with L Rizz is also known to have negative rizz if they keep on trying too hard, make awkward jokes, stumble over their words, and fail in their attempt to impress someone. When someone's attempt at rizzing completely backfires, that's when you know that they've got negative rizz.

Now, unfortunately, if your rizz is even worse than negative rizz, then it's labeled Skibidi Ohio Rizz. Meaning that your charisma is utterly trash. It's an insult if someone says that you have Skibidi Ohio Rizz. And you're a straight-up unappealing person if you're an Ohio Rizzler. What lesson did we learn a couple of chapters ago? Maybe watch a few episodes of The Pickup Artist and you'll be able to recognize Skibidi Ohio Rizz.

Nothing good comes out of Ohio, not even rizzlers.

EXAMPLES

Rizz has earned itself a lot of notoriety over the past few years because of its overuse. It's getting clear that Gen-A, even though they popularized this phrase, are quickly getting sick of it and are making fun of it as a way to make this term irrelevant.

There's something called a TikTok Rizz Party, which is nothing but a cringe concatenation of unrelated words and is probably not a real party but has been made meme-famous on account of its corniness.

There's also a rizz 'chin up' prank. This is when a person attempts to fake read their own palm and then move their hand up to touch another person's chin in a way that is seductive and flirtatious. It's considered to be a move from the unspoken rizz moveset.

Another hilarious example of rizz is called Shrek Rizz, which is a reference to a frame from the movie Shrek where he's looking up, eyebrows raised, face all seductive. The accidentally flirtatious way he's captured mid-frame is known as Shrek Rizz.

If you flirt with someone on the popular online video chatroom called Omegle, it's called Omegle Rizz. Funnily enough, pickup artists who work full-time on their Omegle Rizz have background lighting, multiple cameras, and entire video sketches with which they digitally rizz up an unsuspecting person, causing hilarity to ensue.

Rizz is such a rich goldmine that every sub-set of rizz has its own name.

Do you have low iron? Because every time I get up too fast I always end up falling for you. That's low iron rizz.

Are you French? Because Eiffel for you. That's French rizz. Merci.

You're a 3 because you need 2 realize I'm the 1 made 4 you. That's some corny ass math rizz.

Girl, if you were a basketball, I'd never pass so I can keep you all to myself. That hilarious example of L Rizz is called basketball rizz.

Rizz is more about an entire generation refusing to take themselves too seriously. Gone are the days when seducing someone meant intensely staring at them from across the bar in an attempt to appear mysterious. I mean, the guy from The Pickup Artist literally went by the name Mystery. Nah. That's not how they do it anymore.

You go up to a girl, knowing full well that this can end up with you making a clown out of yourself, and you raise your eyebrow, bite your lower lip, rub your hands together, and say, "Girl, mathematics is all wrong. They keep talking about x and y when they should be talking about u and i." That's some algebra rizz for all you rizzlers.

EIGHTEEN

SIGMA
WHEN ALPHA WON'T DO

IN THE 1970S, David Mech, a famous American biologist, was observing wolves in captivity. In these settings, he noticed that wolves formed hierarchical structures, which led Mech to coin terms like alpha and beta for the dominant and submissive wolves in the pack. However, this observation was based on wolves in unnatural conditions, i.e., captivity, where unrelated groups of wolves were put together. This fostered competition between them and caused a rigid hierarchical structure to form.

Later on, Mech discovered that the wolf packs are not hierarchical but more like family units consisting of parents and offspring. In these natural environments, wolves do not form dominance-based hierarchies. Instead, they operate like human families. Mech noticed there was no need for them to fight for alpha status in their natural habitats.

And so, in 1999, he publicly debunked his own original findings, clarifying that the concept of alpha wolves was misleading and not factually true. He emphasized that he had mistaken the parental guidance of parent wolves guiding children wolves to be alpha behavior. Since then, he has very aggressively advocated removing the alpha terminology from scientific discussions as well as social ones.

Unfortunately for Mech, however, the damage was already done.

People were already starting to use terms like alphas to denote the best of the best and betas to describe submissive people, not knowing that the entire premise behind these terms was flawed and debunked by the same guy who proposed it in the first place.

But does slang always stick with what's right and veer away from what's wrong?

Hell no.

Especially the far-right manosphere on the internet.

Despite the hierarchy being debunked, the manosphere comprised of toxic figures like Andrew Tate still cling to the concept of alpha and beta males. Naturally, since the hyperbolic term of alpha wasn't enough for them, they had to come up with another one.

It's flawed premises all the way down.

ORIGINS

Vox Day, a far-right writer, coined the term sigma in 2010, stating that sigmas were a level higher than alphas, and that they did not care about the social game and yet won it anyway. He basically proposed that sigmas were better than alpha males. Self-reliant lone wolves who don't need any validation.

The term was naturally picked up by the manosphere, a

network of online spaces focused on male identity intersecting with pick-up artist culture and misogynistic forums.

Thankfully, despite its dark origins, the term did not remain confined to far-right circles for long. The Gen-A adopted it due to its broad appeal on social media. How broad? Well, in 2023, the hashtag #sigma gained 46 billion views on TikTok alone, and primarily because it allowed them to talk about this in a semi-ironic way.

DEFINITION

In a modern context, sigmas are individuals who operate outside of social and conventional norms. Unlike the more extroverted alpha males, sigmas are quiet, work in silence, hustle on their own, and are introverted. They prefer solitude and independence. They are very self-reliant, extremely mysterious, and more often than not, because of these antisocial traits, are the butt of Gen-A and Gen-Z jokes while being oblivious to the fact that they're being made fun of.

The sigma male, although portrayed as a cooler, more stoic version of an alpha male, is basically the incel's way of self-ascribing nonconventional value to their nonconforming way of life.

The archetype has become associated with pop-culture characters like Tyler Durden, John Wick, Patrick Bateman, Walter White, and so on. The irony runs deep over here because other than Mr. Wick (please don't hurt me), all of these characters are explicit villains in their stories. They're shown as psychopaths, sociopaths, the kind of people who don't care about breaking the law or causing mayhem.

And that's what the whole sigma hierarchy followers glorify and idolize. And it is not a very healthy form of fixation, because no matter how villainous a thing a self-perceived sigma does, they justify it by thinking of themselves as the outcasts who are better than everyone and know better than anyone.

Almost nobody uses the term sigma in its original form these days, and that is a good thing. It's Gen-A's version of showing us that if there's something toxic and deeply troublesome out there, you can eradicate it by meme-ing the hell out of it.

EXAMPLES

While actors such as Ryan Gosling and characters like Tommy Shelby from Peaky Blinders do tend to embody a certain sigma-ness, the more common usage and examples of the word are nonsensical.

If you want to exclaim, you can go, "What the sigma!?" This phrase originates from a viral meme that shows Squidward from SpongeBob Squarepants seemingly saying this phrase.

If you observe someone flirting with a girl, you can say, "Rizzing up the gyatt like a skibidi sigma!"

If someone does something not-so-cool, you can admonish them by saying, "That wasn't very sigma of you." I remember a time when we used to say, "That wasn't very cash money of you." Simpler times, which are long gone.

Sigma can be used to call something cool. For instance, "He's always leaving the party early because he thinks he's such a sigma." Or "I never study but I always pass. I guess I must be a level ten sigma or something."

Whether it's a reflection of societal shifts or just another passing meme trend, the term 'sigma' has certainly left its mark on 2020's culture and Gen-A slang.

NINETEEN
SKIBIDI
THE ALL-ENCOMPASSING GEN-A NOTHINGBURGER

I'M GOING to share something with you, and it's up to you to decide if it's a fever dream or an actual internet phenomenon that's taken the young ones by storm.

In the future, there is a dystopian Ohio-esque world where there's a bizarre war going on between toilet-headed humans (who are called Skibidi Toilets and bear the face of the antagonist from the Half-Life games, G-Man) and the alliance of Cameramen and Speakermen. Each kind of the alliance has a gigantic version of themselves called the Titans.

There's a mind-controlling parasite infecting the Titan Speakerman, which causes the Titan Speakerman to turn on the alliance. Surprise, surprise, the parasite was created by the skibidi toilet called Scientist Toilet.

The alliance expands into TV-headed humanoids, and with their help, Titan Speakerman is cured.

The war wages on between the toilets and the alliance. Throughout the series, both sides one-up each other in a bid for control.

And no, this isn't a ridiculous psilocybin-induced brain child of mine, it is actually a 70-episode-long series developed by a YouTuber named DaFuq!?Boom! The first video in the series was a head emerging from the toilet singing Dom Dom Yes Yes, a viral Turkish song. Since then, this entire skit has evolved into Marvel-level storytelling with endless battles, plot twists, and the deliberate desecration of millennial cultural fixtures like Half-Life and Counter-Strike.

I cannot weep enough.

You know, these videos have literally millions of views, and the demographic of these nonsense videos is kids. Not teenagers. Not young adults. Kids are being exposed to deep level brainrot with toilet-heads, TV-heads, cameramen, and speakermen fighting each other in surreal and exponentially extreme ways that are supposed to be a deep commentary on the virality of internet content and the juxtaposition of old media vs. new media.

Next time someone asks you where the term comes from, you dump this info on them and watch them question your sanity.

This is a disclaimer to all parents out there. The viral Skibidi Toilet show on YouTube, while marketed to kids, is not children-friendly because it contains depictions of war, violence, and aggressive imagery, some of which can be quite unsettling for a kid under 13 years of age.

In fact, there's an actual term called "Skibidi Toilet Syndrome," which is the belief that the Skibidi Toilet series can harm kids by contributing negatively to their mental health.

ORIGINS

It was supposed to be a nonlexical vocab used in scat singing. That's where it likely originated from. But it was popularized by the 2018 Russian rave band Little Big's song Skibidi.

All current songs about skibidi, whether it's the Turkish Biser King mashup called "Skibidi Dom Dom" or the Russian rave version, essentially mean nothing.

And this entire meaninglessness lends irreverence to the word that is skibidi. You might scratch your head, wondering what skibidi means.

DEFINITION

It means nothing. That's the joke, if it can be called that. It means both nothing and everything, depending on how you want to use it. It's a word without boundaries, serving as an all-purpose explanation, a meme reference, a dance beat, and an abstract descriptor for anything, whether in the form of an adjective, or an adverb, or even a noun.

Skibidi can be a feeling if you let it. It can be a state of being. An event can be skibidi, too.

If you want to describe something weird, confusing, and chaotic, you can call it skibidi.

If you want to describe something funny, that's skibidi, too.

It's the ultimate nothingburger, a term that carries immense cultural weight while simultaneously being completely empty.

Adam Aleksic, the Etymology Nerd, said in a TikTok video that skibidi doesn't have a set definition but can be used as an adjective anywhere. He added that it's not just a random cluster of letters. It follows the phonotactical rules of how words are put together in the English language. These words are known as pseudo-words. They're meaningless but recognizable as words and can be pronounced.

EXAMPLES

There's a popular content creator named Yasin Cengiz on TikTok. He's got a very distinct look. He dances to Bister King's Turkish Skibidi mashup song while shaking his pot belly to it. That's the entire thing. He just shakes his belly up and down while the song plays "Skibidi dom, dom, dom, yes, yes, yes, yes."

Would you be interested in knowing how many followers this guy has? And how many times his videos have been liked? Just out of curiosity?

Okay. He's got 16 million followers who have liked his videos a total of 223 million times. It's variations of the same video of him dancing to the same song. And yet that somehow qualifies for virality.

In fact, his monotonous and low-effort dance remains a popular trend to this day, and thousands of people mimic his moves to the same soundtrack.

Since this word does not have a specific or serious meaning, it can be used in an array of examples, and it's a very rare case where any use is legitimately the right use.

You can say, "We all did the skibidi dance at the party to Biser King," and you'd have used it right.

"That shawarma was the most skibidi thing I've eaten this week," and it'd imply that the shawarma was either the best thing you ate or the worst thing you ate. It's like Schroedinger's Cat; just replace the cat with skibidi toilet.

If you want to denote someone as having good rizz, you can tell them that they have "that skibidi rizz."

However, this does not mean that any and all uses of skibidi will make contextual sense. The popular phrase, "That is so fanum tax skibidi toilet Ohio rizzler," means absolutely nothing at all.

But if you use it wisely and sparingly, skibidi can be a beautiful word for self-reflection, affirmation, complimenting someone, and surprising a loved one.

The rise of words like skibidi underscores the evolution of slang in the internet era. Words don't have to have strict meanings; rather, the less they mean, the better.

Just like skibidi, it can be anything, anywhere, at any time.

It's funny, playful, and just weird enough to make it interesting. And probably that's why it's perfect.

Like you.

You're pretty skibidi, you know that?

Language Shaming-CEO Ousted After E-mail Leak

New York, NY— Richard Cashmore, the controversial CEO of The Hip Company Inc., has been fired after the public leak of the inflammatory emails that he was exchanging with Senior Manager, Blake Balderdash. The emails revealed a targeted plan to encourage older employees to resign. Cashmore's email, mistakenly sent to all employees instead of just his co-conspirator, exposed a strategic initiative called GYATT to replace the senior staff of the company with younger talent by fostering a workplace culture difficult for older employees to navigate and understand.

The GYATT initiative was initially intended as a legal workaround to avoid age discrimination lawsuits. It involved saturating The Hip Company's office culture with Gen-A slang and technology-heavy workshops that Cashmore and Balderdash believed would frustrate older employees to the point of voluntarily quitting.

Cashmore's email described older employees with derogatory descriptors such as 'dead weight' and openly mocked their age-related issues. He likened their presence to 'a ball and chain' that the company needed to 'cut loose.' Furthermore, the CEO made explicit references to certain individuals such as senior employees Phyllis Hardwater and Bob Pasqua.

Following the email leak, the backlash was immediate. Within hours, social media was flooded with reactions from the company's employees, former staff, and the general public, calling for the CEO to be fired. Many former employees recounted their experiences working under Cashmore's leadership. By the end of the business week, hashtags such as #GYATTgate and #CashmoreMeOutside were trending across X, Facebook, and LinkedIn.

Under intense pressure, the company's board of directors held an emergency meeting, shortly after which they released a statement that confirmed that both Cashmore and Balderdash had been terminated effective immediately.

The Hip Company Inc. is committed to fostering a respectful and inclusive workplace," the board's statement read. "The recent conduct displayed by Mr. Cashmore and Mr. Balderdash falls far below our standards, and we believe that this decision is necessary to protect the integrity of our organization and safeguard our interests from threats within.

The leaked email has spurred severe legal repercussions, with multiple current and former employees filing complaints against alleged age discrimination, harassment, and hostile work environment. Legal experts suggest that the company will face significant litigation challenges in the coming months, with potential settlements costing the company millions of dollars.

Cashmore, on the other hand, has remained defiant. In a follow-up email sent shortly before his dismissal, he doubled down on his comments, vowing to fight any lawsuits "tooth and nail" and resisting the "woke-mind virus" that was bent on "canceling him."

Industry analysts say that the incident is emblematic of broader issues around generational diversity in the workplace. "What we see happening is an extreme case of tension between younger and older workers, but the issue of managing generational shifts in the workplace is real and increasingly common," said Miriam Godwell, a workplace DEI culture expert. "The way The Hip Company Inc. handled it is going to serve as a cautionary tale for CEOs everywhere. Cancellation is very real, people."

For The Hip Company Inc., the fallout has been extremely swift and intense. The company's shares dropped 5% by the end of trading, with insiders reporting a morale crisis as the company faces reputation damage, pending lawsuits, and a sudden leadership vacuum.

As the company navigates this scandal, questions linger about the long-term impact of Cashmore's tenure, and whether the company will be able to recover from what is now being called one of the most egregious corporate missteps in recent memory.

GLOSSARY

We can try to be exhaustive with the terms that Gen-A uses, but that would involve afflicting oneself with brainrot on account of internet overuse, even if it is for research. There is so much slang that is being birthed on any given day that it's downright impossible to note down all the words that are being used by the Gen-A.

So, I wrote about the most popular ones.

However, some other terms that I mentioned in this chapter deserve an honorary mention. They're not as popular as the ones that had entire chapters allocated to them, but they're still commonly used by the Gen-A demographic.

1. **Ate.** A term used to express admiration or praise for someone who's excelled at something. When Sza wore that amazing dress at the VMAs, Sza ate and left no crumbs.
2. **Baby Gronk.** A nickname given to a young athlete who's being hyped up as a future football player with exaggerated claims about their potential.

3. **Beige Flag.** A phrase that is used to draw attention to the quirky and neutral traits of partners that may or may not be deal breakers or deal makers, as opposed to red or green flags.

4. **Caught in 4k.** When someone's caught red-handed, they're caught in 4k, and with most phones being able to record 4k videos, the implication is not that far-fetched.

5. **Delulu.** This playful term means someone being delusional or having unrealistic expectations about something. It's often used when someone's out of touch with reality.

6. **FR**. An acronym for "for real" used to express sincerity and agreement.

7. **All Fax, No Printer.** This playful expression emphasizes the truth of something. It's comparable to saying "Just the facts" or "nothing but the truth."

8. **Failmarriage.** A term used to describe a marriage in free fall where the couple decides to stay together, such as the marriage between Shiv and Tom in HBO's Succession.

9. **Gatekeeping.** A term that denotes withholding information or access to something, especially within toxic fandoms.

10. **Girl Dinner.** A humorous way to describe a meal made up of small snacks that girls eat in lieu of an actual dinner.

11. **Girl Math.** A phrase that justifies purchases with unconventional logic on account of subjective math taking place in the girl's head, i.e., girl math.

12. **Glow Up.** A positive transformation in appearance and confidence, usually after a long time, such as pre and post-puberty.

13. **Glazing.** When you overhype something that's not worthy of all this attention, you're effectively glazing it.

14. **Hold this L/Take the L.** Telling someone to accept their loss (or L) with some grace.

15. **Ijbol.** An acronym for "I just burst out laughing" nowadays being used instead of LMAO, LOL, or ROFL.

16. **It's Giving**. When something exudes an energy or a specific vibe, it gives that vibe. So, for instance, "Stranger Things is giving Twin Peak vibes," or when you see autumn roll around, you can say, "It's giving Twilight."

17. **Lewk.** An intentional misspelling of the word 'look', lewk refers to a very fashionable look.

18. **Mid.** Something that's neither top tier nor bottom tier, and is just mundane, boring, a 5 out of 10. An underwhelming mid.

19. **Mother/Mommy.** A term used to express sexual and/or platonic admiration for a powerful female figure such as Lady Dimetrescu from Resident Evil.

20. **Periodt.** This word emphasizes the end of a discussion, underscoring the finality of a point with the word 'periodt.' It's also intentionally misspelled and the 't' is to be spoken.

21. **Rent-Free**. When someone obsesses over something in a way that it occupies their mind without effort, it's said that it's living rent-free in their head.

22. **Shooketh.** An exaggerated form of being shocked or surprised. It's just the word shook role-playing as a medieval character at a Renn Faire.

23. **Vibe Check.** When you assess the mood or energy of a situation, you're checking its vibe. If it's a person in question, if they're cool, then they pass the vibe

check. If they're not cool, then they fail the vibe check
and lose a hundred thousand aura points.

24. **Yap.** In 2024, you don't gab, blabber, or chatter. You
yap. Yapping refers to talking a lot. And those who
cannot stop are called yappers.

Hopefully, armed with these phrases, you'll find yourself better
equipped to deal with the ever-evolving language of the internet's youngest generation. While new phrases and words are
constantly being born from the chaotic corners of Reddit, Instagram, and TikTok, these core terms will help you chart the
waters of the Gen-A slang without getting too lost in the ocean
of brainrot.

MESSAGE FROM THE AUTHOR

Got thoughts? Drop a review for *Brainrot*

You've reached the end of the book, but not the end of the brainrot. You're now empowered to start eavesdropping on those Gen Alpha kiddies out in the wild, trying to decode their *vibe-checking* lingo. Well, now's your chance to share your expertise! If you managed to survive reading through the chaos of brainrot and emerged with your sanity intact, leave a review! You could be the reason someone picks a book that makes their brain fizz like soda.

Click or Scan

Printed in Great Britain
by Amazon